RUSSIAN PRONUNCIATION

RUSSIAN
PRONUNCIATION

A PRACTICAL COURSE

DENNIS WARD, M.A.

LECTURER IN RUSSIAN
UNIVERSITY OF EDINBURGH

OLIVER AND BOYD

EDINBURGH: TWEEDDALE COURT

LONDON: 39A WELBECK STREET, W.1

FIRST PUBLISHED 1958

PRINTED IN GREAT BRITAIN BY
ROBERT CUNNINGHAM AND SONS LTD., ALVA
FOR OLIVER AND BOYD LTD., EDINBURGH

CONTENTS

ACKNOWLEDGEMENTS

I WISH to thank Miss S. Millar and Miss B. Morton, Secretary-Typists in the Department of Modern Languages in the University of Edinburgh, for under-taking the typing of this work. I wish also to thank Mr David Abercrombie, Reader in Phonetics and Head of the Department of Phonetics in the University of Edinburgh, who not only supplied the foreward to this book but also suggested a number of improvements and called my attention to typographical errors which I had overlooked. Any faults that remain in this book are my own responsibility.

D. W.

FOREWORD

THE English learner of Russian is faced with formidable problems of pronunciation: in fact there is no doubt that phonetically Russian is among the most difficult languages of Europe. It is true, of course, that nothing can take the place of oral instruction. Nevertheless the beginner, especially when adult, can obtain inestimable help from a work such as the present. Mr Ward is an experienced teacher and an able phonetician, and he has written a book which is a thoroughly reliable and practical guide through the phonetic complexities of the language, admirably concise but everywhere perfectly clear. I have accepted with much pleasure Messrs Oliver and Boyd's invitation to contribute a foreword to it.

An unusual feature of the book lies in the phonetic notation employed. This constitutes a matter of considerable interest, both from the general phonetic and the pedagogical point of view. There is always a problem of notation in the teaching of the pronunciation of a language which, in its normal written form, uses a script which is different from that used for the learner's mother tongue. It is not possible to do without phonetic transcription; but which of the two scripts, in such a situation, should be made its basis (for a phonetic notation can be created on the basis of any writing system)? To take the case of the English learner of Russian: should the phonetic transcription of Russian words and sentences be presented to him in a notation based on the Roman alphabet, or in one based on the Cyrillic alphabet? There is much to be said for both solutions. The first alternative is the more usual one, and well-known works such as those by Trofimov and Jones, or by Boyanus, for example, make use of the alphabet of the International Phonetic Association, which of course has a Roman basis. Mr Ward has here adopted the second alternative, and this is the first time, I believe, that a phonetic notation based on the Cyrillic alphabet has been put forward for learners of Russian in this country (although considerable use of such a notation, in various forms, has been made in the Soviet Union). The present is a time when a great deal of experimentation is taking place in the use of different types of phonetic notation for all purposes, including language teaching, and phoneticians will welcome Mr Ward's innovation; we may expect to learn much from it.

No book of this kind should be expected to be easy, but time spent on mastering the notation and working through the exercises will be amply repaid.

DAVID ABERCROMBIE

EDINBURGH, *June* 1958

INTRODUCTION

Most students of Russian begin their study of the language after leaving school—either at a university or in the armed forces or privately. They are obliged to cover in a short time that which, in the study of Russian or any other language at school, would occupy several years. As a result of this they and their teachers usually have little time to devote to a detailed study and practice of Russian pronunciation and must treat this subject in broad outline, perhaps returning to a finer study when the fundamentals of Russian grammar have been assimilated. Moreover, in study-ing Russian pronunciation, many beginners have either little time or little inclination to learn the necessary symbols of the Inter-national Phonetic Alphabet: they are already struggling with the novelty of Cyrillic characters.

The Russian alphabet can be easily adapted to serve as a means for recording the pronunciation of the language. Indeed, Soviet phoneticians habitually use this modified Cyrillic alphabet in works on Russian pronunciation. The advantage of this system for the foreign beginner in Russian is that he is absolved from the necessity of learning another set of letters, the modifications of the Russian alphabet being readily comprehensible, and it is for that reason that the system is used in this book. The Cyrillic letters used to indicate sounds are always enclosed in square brackets and in the examples the normal spelling of words is given first, then the phonetic transcription (in modified Cyrillic) follows in square brackets and this is followed by the meaning in English, printed in italics, thus: юбка [йу́пкъ] *skirt*.

A brief glance at the book will show that it is not intended for the specialist in phonetics: it is primarily intended for the beginner in Russian, though the more advanced student will find useful material in it, especially perhaps in the final chapters. Since the book is not intended for phoneticians, technical terminology has been kept to a minimum and only the briefest description of the organs of speech is given in Chapter 1. Moreover, for the same reason, the sounds are not described in a systematic sequence (systematic, that is, from the point of view of general phonetics) but in a sequence determined for the most part by degree of difficulty. The exercises, too, have been made 'progressive', as far as this is possible. This is to say that examples involving sounds which are described in subsequent chapters are kept to a minimum. Thus, no 'soft' consonants other than [ʧ] are used in the examples in the early chapters before soft consonants in general have been described. It is, however, impossible to adhere to this system throughout, without resorting to somewhat outlandish examples, so that here and there there are examples involving sounds which are not described until later. This does not invalidate the general principle.

No description of the sounds of a language can perfectly convey the actual acoustic impressions received when listening to the language. The student must, therefore, bear in mind that, without hearing Russian sounds produced by a native speaker or a teacher with a good accent, he is unlikely to produce Russian sounds perfectly himself, no matter how many and how fine the descriptions he reads. He must continually verify what he learns by listening to spoken Russian.

Once he has learnt the sounds of Russian, the student has still not overcome all his problems in learning to pronounce Russian. There is the very important problem of what happens when consonants of certain types come together. A special section of the book is devoted to this subject and it is one which the student— even the student who already feels he has mastered the sounds of Russian—would do well to read thoroughly, since the proper formations in these cases are an essential part of the correct pronunciation of Russian.

It will be seen from the way in which the examples are disposed that the essential principle is 'from the letter to the sound', i.e. the student is taught what is the phonetic value of the written word. Again, this has been done because the book is not a work for the phonetician but one for the general student of Russian. Russian spelling is not, in many points, a very reliable guide to the pronunciation of the language. The chapters dealing with the individual sounds, containing, as they do, information about the representation of these sounds in written Russian, together with the following section on the juxtaposition of consonants, should help the student over the basic difficulties. There are, however, anomalies —exceptions to the 'rules' given in these earlier chapters—and so the last chapters of the book are devoted to an elucidation of these anomalies, preceded by a summary of some of the more important points in earlier chapters. A few passages for practice and application of the 'rules' are given in an appendix.

Throughout the relevant parts of the book the 'adaptive' method supplements, where necessary, the ordinary descriptive method. This is to say that, in addition to a simple description of the manner in which a sound is formed, instructions are given to the student for *adapting* or modifying a native speech-sound or one of the Russian sounds already learnt in order to make an easier approach to the new sound being treated. The type of pronunciation of English which is taken as a basis in this respect is that which has come to be known among phoneticians and others as 'Received Pronunciation' (RP). It is the type of pronunciation used by those who have been educated at the English public schools, by the families of such people and by many thousands more who have not been at such schools but who have learnt this type of pronunciation at home, at university or from their professional or social contacts. A typical example of RP is the pronunciation of any newsreader on the B.B.C. national services.

Reference is also made to a type of American pronunciation known as General American (GA), since in many instances the instructions given to RP speakers for adapting their native speech-sounds are inappropriate for American students. Remarks have also been included for the benefit of Scots speakers and in this context 'Scots' refers to the type of pronunciation used by educated Scotsmen who have not adopted RP and who, while having no traits of any specific Scots dialect in their pronunciation, quite clearly speak 'with a Scots accent'. It may be wondered why the author, who is not himself a Scot, has troubled to include such remarks, the population of Scotland being only about one fifth of that of England and about one fourteenth that of the United States of America. There are several reasons why this has been done. There are Russian Departments at two of the four Scottish Universities, and there is the possibility that Russian Departments will be established at the other two Scottish Universities, and many, though not all, of the students in those departments are native Scots. Moreover, though the population of Scotland is small, there are many thousands of Scots outside Scotland, among them students and teachers of modern languages. Finally, the few remarks included for the benefit of Scots-speaking students may serve as a small tribute to those Scottish school authorities who have had the foresight to introduce Russian into schools, particularly in Edinburgh, where there has been and is proportionately more interest in Russian in the schools than in possibly any other town in Britain.

1

GENERAL PHONETICS

(a) The Organs of Speech

BEFORE the sounds of the Russian language can be described, it is necessary to describe the functioning of some of the organs of speech. The following description has been kept as brief as possible and is cast in as simple a language as possible. The principal object of this description and the accompanying exercises is to familiarise the student with the operation of the speech-organs.

The lips are used both in the formation of vowels and in the formation of consonants. In the formation of the consonants in *pie*, *by*, *my*, for example, the lips are fully closed for a short time and are then opened quickly. Observe in a mirror the action of the lips in pronouncing the words *apart*, *about*, *amok* and note how in all three words the lips are at first open for the initial vowel-sound, then close briefly for the consonants *p*, *b*, *m* respectively, before opening again for the second vowel. These three consonants have in common a complete closure of the two lips and are distinguished from each other by other features: the presence or absence of voice, the issuing of air through the nose.

In the formation of the initial consonants of *file* and *vile* both the lower lip and the teeth are used. The lips are slightly parted and the upper teeth are just in contact with the inside of the lower lip. Friction is produced as the air passes between the lower lip and the upper teeth and this is the quality that distinguishes *f* and *v* from all other sounds.

In careful pronunciation the lips adopt a variety of positions in the formation of vowel-sounds. Thus, the lips may make a round shape, as when pronouncing the vowel in *soon*; or they may be spread wide, forming a slit-like aperture, as in the pronunciation of the vowel in *cease*; or they may be opened wide, without being rounded, as in the pronunciation of the first vowel in *father* (RP and

GA[1]); or they may adopt a position somewhere between these extremes. In hurried or careless pronunciation the positions adopted by the lips in the formation of different vowel-sounds may vary only slightly, if at all. The really distinctive positions are to be observed only in careful pronunciation.

EXERCISE 1. Pronounce the following words very carefully, observing the movement of the lips in a mirror: *soon, home, lawn, father* (first vowel), *hat, get, day, cease*. Notice how the lips change their position and hence the shape of the opening as the different words are pronounced. Now pronounce only the vowel-sounds from these words, first separately and then in one long glide from *oo* (as in *soon*) to *ea* (as in *cease*). The movement of the lips into different positions should now be even more obvious.

It will be noticed that in pronouncing the vowels represented by *o* in *home* and *ay* in *day* the lips do not stay in one position but start in one position and then glide into another position. This is because the vowels in these words are not in fact simple vowels but 'glides', starting in the position of one vowel and moving immediately into the position of another vowel. They are known as 'diphthongs'.

Scots speakers will probably find that in pronouncing the vowels in *home* and *day* their lips do stay in one position. This is because such speakers pronounce not a diphthong but a simple vowel in such words. Speakers of GA will usually find only a very slight movement of the lips or none at all in pronouncing these vowels.

Even in hurried speech, when the lip positions for the various vowels hardly differ, the vowels are still quite distinct from each other. This is because the tongue also plays a part in forming vowel-sounds. Indeed, the part played by the tongue must be more important than the part played by the lips, since, as has just been stated, the vowels remain distinct from each other even when the lips are almost inactive.

EXERCISE 2. Say the vowel in *soon* and then the vowel in *lawn*, paying particular attention to the sensation of position and shape of the tongue. Say the same two vowels in reverse order. It will be found that in pronouncing these vowels the tongue is arched (the sensation is very apparent in the pronunciation of *oo*), that the tongue moves down as first *oo* and then *aw* is pronounced and

[1] RP = 'Received Pronunciation' of English, GA = General American (see Introduction).

that, conversely, it moves up again as first *aw* and then *oo* is pronounced. Moreover, the lower jaw moves up and down with the tongue. Now repeat this process with the vowels in *cease* and *hat*. Again the tongue will be found to move up and down (and with it the lower jaw) but this time it is clearly the front of the tongue which is moving up and down, whereas in performing the first part of this exercise it was actually the back of the tongue which moved up into an arched position and then down from this position: say first *ea* and then *oo* and notice the very distinct sensation of change from front to back in the arching of the tongue[1] and also a very distinct movement of the lower jaw.

Some students may find, when trying the foregoing exercise, that they tend to make the lip movements very precisely and these lip movements make difficult for them the perception of the movement of the tongue. They should try to perform the exercise in a lazy manner, i.e. with the lips as inactive as possible. Lazy articulation with the lips will not make any fundamental difference to the movement of the tongue in forming vowel-sounds. The difference between the tongue-position for *ea* and that for *oo* may be more readily apparent than the vertical differences in the tongue-position but with some repetition of the exercise these vertical differences should also become perceptible.

Vowels in the formation of which the front of the tongue is raised (no matter how little, as in the case of the vowel in *hat*) are known as 'front' vowels, while those in the formation of which the back of the tongue is raised or the tongue is kept as flat as possible are known as 'back' vowels. Vowels for which the tongue is raised high are known as 'close' vowels, those for which the tongue is low in the mouth being known as 'open' vowels. Between the extreme 'close' position and the extreme 'open' position there is an indefinite number of intermediate positions.

EXERCISE 3. Say the vowels used in Exercise 1, paying particular attention to the position of the tongue (if necessary, use lazy lip articulation). Say the vowels separately first and then in one long glide, without any break between them. The back of the tongue will be found to move down from *oo* (in *soon*) to *a* (in *father*) and then the front of the tongue to move up from *a* (in *hat*) to *ea* (in *cease*), passing through an indefinite number of positions between

---

[1] Scots speakers will find that in pronouncing *oo* they raise not the back of the tongue but a point somewhat further forward.

these extremes. Now say the vowels in the reverse sequence and notice how the movement of the tongue is also reversed.

The teeth alone are not normally used to produce speech sounds but are used in conjunction with other speech organs. We have seen how the upper teeth are used to make a slight contact with the inside of the lower lip in the formation of the initial consonants of *file* and *vile*. The teeth are used as a point of contact for the tongue in the production of some speech sounds. Thus, the sound represented by *th* in *thin* is made with the tip of the tongue against the back of the upper teeth, or between the teeth, and in many languages sounds similar to English *n*, *t*, *d* are also made with the tip of the tongue against the back of the upper teeth.

In English, however, the sounds *n*, *t*, *d* are made with the tip of the tongue against the teeth-ridge. This is the bony, convex part of the roof of the mouth just behind the upper teeth. Behind the teeth-ridge the roof of the mouth sweeps up in an arch, which continues to the back of the mouth. This arched part of the roof of the mouth is the palate, the front part forming the hard palate, the rear part forming the soft palate. The respective hardness and softness of the hard and soft palates can be tested with the tip of the tongue.[1]

The hard and soft palates are used as points of contact against which various consonants are made with the tongue. It is the tip or the front of the tongue or both together which form contact or near-contact against the hard palate while the back of the tongue forms contact or near-contact against the soft palate.

EXERCISE 4. (*a*) Say *take*, *nook*, *done* and notice how the initial consonants are formed with the tip of the tongue against the teeth-ridge.

(*b*) Say *sheep*, *measure* and notice how the consonants represented respectively by *sh* and *s* are made with the front part of the tongue against the palate.

(*c*) Say *corn*, *gun* and notice how the initial consonants are formed with the back of the tongue against the soft palate.

The soft palate or velum ends in a little flap of flesh known as the

---

[1] It is an easy enough matter to examine with the tip of the tongue the shape and texture of the roof of the mouth as far back as the beginning of the soft palate. With a very little practice it is possible to move the tip of the tongue back along the soft palate—and with considerable practice even beyond the soft palate on to the back of the throat.

uvula. This can be seen in a mirror and, with a little practice, it can be felt with the tip of the tongue by curling the tongue over backwards as far as it will go.

Behind the velum is the pharynx, the part of the throat above the wind-pipe. In forming most consonants and vowels the velum is raised against the back wall of the pharynx so that no air can issue through the nose. When the velum is lowered, air can issue through the nose. Sounds produced by air issuing through the nose are known as nasal sounds. Most people are not aware of the lowering and raising of the velum, though they are perfectly capable of making nasal and non-nasal sounds.

EXERCISE 5. Hold the back of the hand just below the nostrils and hum the sound m or n, thus mmmmm... or nnnnn... A steady stream of air can be felt against the back of the hand as long as m or n is hummed. If you are a smoker, light a cigarette, inhale smoke and then, while looking in a mirror, hum m or n. Smoke will be seen issuing from the nostrils. Say bad and then mad keeping the back of the hand below the nostrils, and see if you can detect that there is a puff of air against the hand when mad is pronounced but not when bad is pronounced. Try the same trick with bad and ban and notice that the puff of air felt in the pronunciation of ban comes at the end of the word, whereas the puff of air associated with mad comes at the beginning of the word. Whenever the puff of air is felt issuing from the nose a nasal sound has been made.[1]

The larynx, or voice-box, is situated in the wind-pipe. It consists of supporting tissue and the vocal cords, which are strips of muscle running from front to back in two horizontal bands facing each other. When these two bands are brought together any air that is issuing from the lungs is brought momentarily to a halt before it builds up enough pressure to force the vocal cords apart. The cords then come together again and the whole process is repeated many times a second. The rapid opening and closing of the vocal cords sets up certain vibrations in the air passing from the lungs and these vibrations are heard as 'voice'. If the vocal cords are apart, these vibrations are not produced and no 'voice'

[1] A bad cold in the head may prevent any air at all from issuing through the nose. No puffs of air can be felt and no puffs of smoke seen when one pronounces man: it will sound like bad and so will ban and mad (imagine trying to say ban the bad, mad man with a bad head-cold!)

is heard. The opening and closing in rapid alternation is, in a sense, purely mechanical and cannot be controlled: all that the speaker does is to place the vocal cords in the closed position and the air-stream does the rest. The voluntary placing of the vocal cords in the closed or open position has to be learnt in infancy but with the years we become so used to the movement that we no longer notice any muscular effort nor even, unless attention is particularly called to it, the 'switching on and off' of the voice.

The other speech-organs then produce modifications in the stream of air (with or without voice) issuing from the lungs. The resultant effect is a connected series of speech-sounds. Speech-sounds produced with voice are known as 'voiced' sounds, those without as 'voiceless' sounds. Vowels are usually voiced but some consonants are voiced while others are voiceless. Voiced consonants include, for example, the sounds heard at the beginning of *me, long, good, bad, done.* Voiceless consonants include those heard at the beginning of *seen, sheep, cool, pad, ton.*

Many English speakers frequently pronounce voiced consonants as only partially voiced: they may begin or end a voiced consonant without voice so that only the end or beginning respectively is voiced properly. It is important in Russian pronunciation to make voiced sounds completely voiced throughout.

Exercise 6. Put a finger in each ear and hum *mmm...* and then *nnn...* All that can be heard in either case is a droning noise—the voice. Now hum *lll...* (not a series of separate *l*'s but one long *l*). Again, all that can be heard is the droning of the voice. Hum *zzz...* The drone is still there but now there is also a faint hissing noise behind the drone: this is the friction which gives the sound *z* its special quality. Still keeping the fingers in the ears, make a long *sss...* All that can be heard now is a hissing noise: there is no drone of voice because *sss...* is a voiceless sound.

Exercise 7. Repeat the pronunciation of *sss...* and *zzz...*, making quite sure that the drone of the voice is heard all through *zzz...* and that the sound does not begin or end with a slight voiceless hiss. If it does, then it is only partially voiced. If the voiceless hiss comes at the beginning, practise saying *nnnzzz...* without any pause between the *nnn* and the *zzz*. If the voiceless hiss comes at the end practise saying *zzznnn*. Reduce the *nnn* at either end until only fully voiced *zzz* is left.

Exercise 8. Put a finger in each ear and say the sound represented by *d* in *do*. The drone of the voice will be heard very briefly as *d* is pronounced. Now say the sound represented by *t* in *too*. This time all that will be heard will be a short puff or a faint click. The *d* is voiced, the *t* is voiceless. Repeat the exercise, making sure that the drone of the voice is heard throughout the brief duration of *d*. Alternatively, say *nnnd*. This should assure that the *d* is voiced. (In saying *nnnt*, with the fingers in the ears, it will be noticed that the drone suddenly stops and a puff of air is heard at the end.) Carry out a similar exercise with *mmmb*, ending with simply a fully voiced *b*.

(*b*) STRESS

When one pronounces the word *window*, one exerts more 'force' in uttering the first syllable than in uttering the second syllable: *WINdow*. Conversely, the second syllable of *before* is pronounced with greater force than is the first syllable—*beFORE*. A syllable pronounced with greater force than other syllables in a word is known as the 'stressed' syllable and the vowel in it is the 'stressed' vowel. The other syllables and vowels in the word are 'unstressed'. The noun 'stress' is used to denote the greater force used in pronouncing a stressed vowel. In short words in English it is usually necessary to distinguish only stressed and unstressed syllables. In longer words, however, one of the unstressed syllables may in fact be somewhat more heavily stressed than the other unstressed syllables while not being as heavily stressed as the syllable bearing the main stress, i.e. the stressed syllable properly speaking. Thus, in the word *contemporaneous* the stress is on the syllable -*ran*- (pronounced, of course, like the word *rain*), while the other syllables are, in comparison with this one, unstressed. However, it is clear that one unstressed syllable, namely -*tem*-, stands out more sharply than the other unstressed syllables: this syllable is said to be in the position of secondary stress, or to be under secondary stress.

It is convenient to have some means of indicating which is the stressed syllable. An acute accent placed over the vowel of the stressed syllable is a simple and convenient way of indicating stress: *wíndow*, *befóre*. When necessary a secondary stress may be indicated by a grave accent: *contèmporáneous*, *excitabílity*.

Russian, like English, has stressed and unstressed syllables and also syllables with secondary stress. In this book, when words of only one syllable are taken as examples or occur in sentences, the stress-mark (i.e. the acute accent) is not usually printed: it is to be understood that the vowel, being the only one in the word, must be stressed.[1]

[1] A few monosyllabic words in Russian—and a very few of more than one syllable—are never stressed. This and similar phenomena are dealt with in Chapter 11.

2

SOME EASY CONSONANTS AND VOWELS

(a) Twelve Consonants

None of the consonants in this chapter should present any special difficulty to the English-speaking student, since most of them are very like English sounds and only in a few cases are there special points to be observed.[1]

[й]

The consonant [й] is like the y in English yield. The sound is a 'glide', i.e. the tongue takes up the position more or less for Russian [и] (see below) and then glides immediately into the following vowel without making the [и] into a separate syllable. It is quite weakly articulated in Russian and tends to disappear when it occurs between two vowels and the second is unstressed. The English y-sound is sometimes pronounced with quite audible friction, which is quite wrong in Russian, except in the special circumstances described in Chapter 5.

Exercise 9. With a finger in each ear pronounce some English words beginning with y—youth, yield, your, etc. Listen carefully to see if you can detect any slight hissing with the initial consonant (it will be heard as a sort of after-effect to the y before the vowel is heard). If there is any trace of hissing, the y is being produced with friction and you should practise making the sound with the tongue relaxed: try, as it were, to be careless about the production of y, so as to make it into an adequate substitute for Russian [й]. It is not at all otiose to practise this relaxed articulation for Russian [й] even if there is no trace of friction in your pronunciation of English y.

The consonant [й] occurs mostly as an initial sound or between vowels. The letter й, used to indicate [й] as the second part of a diphthong (Chapter 8), indicates consonantal [й] in only a very

---

[1] Words illustrating the usage of the consonants in this section are given in the exercises in the second section of the chapter and in the following chapters.

few words, e.g. йод (also иод) [йот] *iodine*, район [район] *region*, майор [майóр] *major*. Otherwise [й] is indicated by one of the vowel-letters е, ю, я, which, at the beginning of a word and after another vowel-letter, ъ or ь, have the value of [й] followed by the appropriate vowel. Before the vowel [и] the consonant [й] occurs only rarely, as in чьи [чйи] *whose*, so that the letter и usually represents simply the vowel [и].[1]

[б], [м], [г], [ч]

The four consonants [б], [м], [г], [ч] are respectively like the initial consonants in the English words *bore, more, gore, chore*. The last of these, [ч], is actually a 'soft' consonant but since it is indistinguishable from English *ch* (as in *chore*) and presents no difficulties whatever it is included here and not in the chapters on soft consonants. These four consonants are represented in spelling as follows:

[б] by the letter б and also occasionally by the letter п (if this letter is followed by a letter representing one of the voiced consonants [б], [д], [з], [ж], [г], [д'], [з'], [г']);

[м] by the letter м;

[г] by the letter г[2] and also occasionally by the letter к (if this letter is followed by a letter representing one of the voiced consonants [б], [д], [з], [ж], [г], [б'], [д'], [з']);

[ч] by the letter ч and also by the letter щ, which, in the pronunciation of some Russians, represents a soft [ш'] followed by [ч].[3]

[ф], [в], [с], [з]

The four consonants [ф], [в], [с], [з] are respectively like the initial consonants in the English words *fog, vogue, soon, zoo*. A particular point to note is that, whereas English *v* and *z* (as in *vogue* and *zoo* respectively) are sometimes only partially voiced, Russian [в] and [з] must be fully voiced whenever they occur.

EXERCISE 10. With a finger in each ear make a prolonged *v* and then a prolonged *z*, trying to detect whether, in either case, there is the slightest trace of hissing unaccompanied by the humming of

---

[1] See, however, Chapter 10, and note that after ш, ж and ц the letter и represents [ы].

[2] Before к and ч in some words the letter г represents the sound [x] or the sound [x'] (see Chapter 10).

[3] The sound [ш'] is described in Chapter 7.

the voice. If there is, then the sound being tested is not completely voiced and the student should then practise initiating the *v* and *z* with *m* and *n* respectively (if *v* and *z* are found to be voiceless at the beginning) or concluding *v* and *z* with *m* and *n* respectively (if *v* and *z* are found to be voiceless at the end). The *m* and *n* should then be gradually reduced until only fully voiced *v* and *z* are left.

These four consonants are represented in spelling as follows: [ф] by the letter ф and also by the letter в (if this letter occurs at the end of a word or is followed by a letter representing a voiceless consonant);

[в] by the letter в and also occasionally by the letter ф (if this letter occurs before a letter representing one of the voiced consonants [б], [д], [з], [ж] or [г] or one of their soft counterparts[1];

[с] by the letter с and also by the letter з (if this letter occurs at the end of a word or is followed by a letter representing a voiceless consonant);

[з] by the letter з and also by the letter с (if this letter occurs before a letter representing one of the voiced consonants [б], [д], [з], [г] or either of the voiced soft consonants [б'] or [г'].

[д], [н]

The nearest sounds in English to the Russian sounds [д] and [н] are *d* and *n* respectively (as in *dog* and *not*). There is, however, this important difference: the English sounds are pronounced with the tip of the tongue touching the teeth-ridge, *whereas the Russian sounds are formed with the tip of the tongue further forward, in the angle where the upper teeth issue from the gum.* The two methods of pronunciation give quite different acoustic effects, so it is important to form Russian [д] and [н] in the correct manner. It is not, however, a difficult matter to do this and though at first one may have to make a conscious effort it is not long before one is making correct Russian [д] and [н] automatically. It is quite helpful to mark every [д] and [н] in a passage for reading aloud, as a reminder that they are *dental* consonants, i.e. formed with the tip of the tongue against the back of the upper teeth.

[д] is represented in spelling by the letter д and also by the

---

[1] The letter ф is not of very common occurrence, so that some of the combinations of ф with another consonant letter will be found but rarely, if at all.

letter т (when, as frequently happens, this letter occurs before a
letter representing one of the voiced consonants [б], [д], [з], [ж]
or [г] or either of the voiced 'soft' consonants [б'] and [г']).

[н] is represented in spelling by the letter н.

[ц]

The sound [ц] is seemingly composed of two sounds, rather like
English *t* (as in *ton*) and *s* (as in *son*) spoken in rapid succession.
This is, in fact, how the sound is formed and it may be compared
with the -*ts* in English *bits* or—a better comparison—in the sentence *take some bits off*, where the *s* is less likely to be prolonged
than in the word *bits* spoken on its own. In Russian [ц] both the
'*t*' element and the '*s*' element are very short: the tongue no sooner
makes the '*t*' position than the '*s*' is sounded and this itself is kept
very short. Indeed, [ц] at the beginning of a word or between
vowels takes up very little more time, if any more at all, than
English *t* in the same positions.

Care must be taken not to let any other sound whatsoever, no
matter how short, intervene between the '*t*' element and the '*s*'
element, i.e. one must not release the tongue from the '*t*'-position
and then say the '*s*', linking them together with what would in
effect be a very short voiceless vowel. The student is most likely
to do this when the consonant [ц] is at the beginning of a word,
since it is in this position that the sequence *ts* does not occur in
English words.[1]

EXERCISE 11. Practise [ц] between two vowels, thus [аца].[2] Remember to keep both elements of [ц] as short as possible. Now
practise the sound without a following vowel—[ац]—taking care
not to prolong the final '*s*' element. Finally, when [аца] and [ац]
and other similar combinations have been thoroughly practised,
make the consonant [ц] with a vowel after it but none before it
—[ца]. Remember that there should be no trace of vowel between
the '*t*' and the '*s*'. If difficulty is experienced in this part of the

[1] There are just a very few exceptions to this statement, namely the
specialised words *tsar, tsarevich, tsarina* (all three of which are more usually pronounced as if spelt with an initial *z*) and *tsetse* (in this word the *s*
after the initial *t* is pronounced by English speakers somewhat longer
than the '*s*' element in Russian [ц]. The word may also be pronounced
as if spelt '*tetse*' (according to D. Jones' *English Pronouncing Dictionary*).

[2] No stress-mark is given, since this is not a 'real' word but merely a
vocable for practice purposes and it is immaterial where the stress is placed.

exercise, start by saying [аца] and then gradually shorten the first [a] until it disappears altogether, leaving only [ца]. Alternatively, you may like to take the word *tsetse* (see footnote 1, page 16) as a starting-point for initial [ц], concentrating on making the *s* as short as possible without, of course, allowing it to lapse altogether.

[ц] is represented in spelling by the letter ц.[1] In a very few words the letter represents a voiced [ц] (like a sequence of very short '*d*' followed by very short '*z*'), as in плацдарм [пладздáрм] *jumping-off ground, base.* The letter combinations тс, дс, тьс may also represent [ц], as in боится [бáйцъ] *fears,* бояться [байáцъ] *to fear,* городской [гърацкóй] *urban.*

(b) THREE VOWELS

[a]

The Russian vowel [a] is different from the sound represented by *a* in such English words as *cat, bad,* etc. The *a* in *cat* has a certain '*e*'-quality about it. (It is frequently not unlike the first part of the Russian vowel [э].) Russian [a], however, has none of this quality. It is more like the *a* heard in North Country pronunciations of such words as *cat, bad,* or the vowel in the French word *chat.* It is more 'open' than the *a* in *cat,* in fact it is a fully 'open' vowel, while still being a 'front' vowel (see Introduction).

Such English words as *eye, my,* etc. contain a diphthong which starts at a point very near to that of Russian [a], proceeding thence in the direction of *i* in English *bit.* Students who are unable to produce [a] by following the description in the preceding paragraph or by imitation should try the following exercise:

EXERCISE 12. Say '*eye*'. Repeat slowly. As the pronunciation is slowed down, i.e. as the word is drawn out, the diphthongal nature of the vowel-sound becomes very evident. Begin to say the word

---

[1] It may seem strange to English-speaking students that what is apparently two sounds should be represented by one letter. It has been pointed out, however, that [ц] differs from a sequence such as *ts* in English: it also differs from the sequence of the sounds roughly corresponding to *t* and *s* in Russian, namely [т] and [с], in being shorter than the sum of these two. Moreover, it should not be so very surprising that there is a single letter ц, since English often represents *ks* (and also *gz*) by the single letter *x*, and in this case there is much less justification for the use of a single letter. Students of German will be familiar with that language's 'equivalent' to Russian [ц], which is also represented by a single letter, namely *z*.

eye very slowly again and this time do *not* go on to the final *i*-element but continue the *a*-element. Practise pronouncing this *a* on its own, making it shorter, until it is simply a short *a*-vowel. Now practise this sound with various consonants both before and after it: [ба], [ма], [са], [ас], [ам], [аба], [маба], [сама], etc.

RP speakers do not, as a rule, find it difficult to avoid using the English *a* (in *cat*) in place of the Russian [a]. They are, however, more inclined to replace the Russian [a] by the vowel heard in RP *half*, or a shortened version of this. Such a pronunciation for Russian *a* is, of course, incorrect. The exercise given above should help towards eradicating this mistake. Some RP speakers, however, use, in such words as *eye*, *my*, a diphthong which starts at a point close to that of their vowel in *half* or the first vowel in their pronunciation of *father*. In such cases Exercise 12 will be of no help.

In order to verify whether his diphthong in *eye*, etc. begins with a sound similar to the *a* in *father*, the student should try the first part of Exercise 12, using, however, the word *fie* instead of *eye*. Having isolated the first part of the diphthong in this word, retaining the initial *f*, he should then add to it the second part of the word *father*, i.e. *-ther*, saying the two elements without a break, as if they were one word. If the resultant combination sounds like a reasonably close approximation to his normal pronunciation of the word *father*, then the vowel of the *a*-type which he has isolated from the diphthong in *fie* will not do for Russian [a]. Such students will have to try to produce a vowel which is, so to speak, 'midway' between their *a* in *cat* and their *a* in *father*.

GA speakers usually pronounce the vowel in *cat* with an *e*-quality, more or less in the RP manner. Such speakers, if unable to produce Russian [a] by imitation or by following the description given in the first paragraph of this section, should also try Exercise 12.

Some Scots speakers also pronounce the vowel in *cat* more or less in the RP manner, some of them going even further in the direction of *e* (as in *get*). They, too, may find Exercise 12 a convenient way of approaching Russian [a]. Many other Scots speakers, however, have a vowel in *cat* (and also in *half* and in the first syllable of *father*) which is very close to Russian [a] and will serve adequately for the Russian sound.

Russian [a] is represented in spelling by the letter a and also by я (which letter denotes also a preceding [й] or a preceding soft consonant).

EXERCISE 13. Practise the following words: час [час] *hour*, сам [сам] *self*, газ [гас] *gas*, да [да] *yes*, нам [нам] *us*, бац [бац] *bang*, я [йа] *I*, яма [йа́мъ] *pit*.

UNSTRESSED [a] AND THE UNSTRESSED VOWEL [ъ]

Unstressed [a] has a similar acoustic quality to stressed [a]. It is, however, not quite as open as stressed [a] and is formed further back though not as far back as the vowel in RP *half*. It is very like the vowel in RP *nut*. Once stressed [a] has been learnt, unstressed [a] will usually arise 'automatically', if the student pronounces unstressed vowels in a somewhat more 'relaxed' manner than stressed vowels.

The unstressed vowel [ъ] is even less open than unstressed [a], though not so far back: in this latter respect it is a 'central' vowel, i.e. the tongue is slightly arched at a point roughly midway along its length. [ъ] sounds very much like the vowel heard at the end of RP *china, villa, borough* and words ending in *-er, -or*, etc. (*over, actor, collar*). Some RP speakers, however, use at the end of such words a vowel like the one they use in *nut*. In order to ascertain which type of vowel the RP speaker uses at the end of *china*, etc., he should perform the following exercise.

EXERCISE 14. Say the word *china*, adding to it a final '*t*', so that you produce a vocable which might be written *china-t*. Try now to isolate the second syllable: (*chi-*)*nat*, i.e. say it on its own while still preserving the quality of the vowel in that syllable. If *-nat* sounds like your pronunciation of *nut* then you will have to use another vowel in place of Russian [ъ]. The best one to use as a starting-point is the vowel used in *bird, heard*, etc. It should, however, be reduced in length, since Russian [ъ] is a short vowel, whereas the vowel in RP *bird, heard*, etc. is quite long.

In words like *nut* GA speakers generally use a vowel which is very like Russian [ъ] and will serve as a substitute for or at least a starting-point from which to obtain Russian [ъ]. Such speakers, in order to obtain unstressed [a] will then have to aim at a vowel which is neither [ъ] nor stressed [a] but something intermediate, that is if they are unable to produce an adequate unstressed [a] simply by 'relaxing' the pronunciation of stressed [a].

Scots speakers usually have no vowel quite like the one heard at the end of RP *china, villa, over*, etc. (see the second paragraph of this section). In the second syllable of such words as *china, colour, actor* they use a vowel like the one they use in *nut* (followed by an *r*-sound if there is a written *r* at the end of the word), whereas in the second syllable of such words as *father, mother* they use a vowel like the one they use in *bit* (followed by an *r*-sound). The vowel which such speakers use in *nut* and also in the second syllable of *china, colour, actor, collar*, etc. (but *not* the one which they use in the second syllable of *father, mother*, etc.) will serve as an adequate substitute for unstressed [a]. To obtain [ъ] they may aim at a vowel which is neither the one in their pronunciation of *net*, nor the one in their pronunciation of *nut* but is intermediate between the two. Alternatively, they may try to make their pronunciation of unstressed [a] even more relaxed—with hardly any opening of the jaws—in order to obtain [ъ].

Both unstressed [a] and [ъ] are represented in spelling by the letters a and o.[1] In positions after the stressed syllable (but *not* before it) the letter я also represents [ъ] (preceded by a soft consonant or [й]).

Having learnt the two vowels, RP students often make the mistake of using them in the wrong place—[ъ] in the place of unstressed [a] and *vice versa*. GA and Scots speakers, if they have learnt the sounds properly, seem less likely to make this mistake.

Unstressed [a] is used in three different positions. The first of these is the syllable *immediately preceding* the stressed syllable. The second position is an unstressed syllable at the beginning of a word *when there is no initial consonant*, whether or not such an unstressed syllable is immediately before the stressed syllable. This does not apply in the case where the vowel is immediately preceded by the final consonant of one of the common prepositions since preposition and following word usually form a phonetic unit in Russian. Thus, одному [аднамý] *to one* but к одному [къднамý] *to one*, одного [аднавó] *of one* but от одного [атъднавó] *from one*.

The third case of the use of unstressed [a] can best be explained in terms of spelling. It happens not infrequently that in positions before the stress, both in single words and in combinations of preposition plus following word (forming a phonetic unit), the letter-combinations aa, ao, oo, oa occur. In such cases each of

---

[1] After the letters ч and щ the letter a in unstressed position before the stressed syllable represents the unstressed vowel [ь] (see Chapter 8).

the two letters represents the unstressed vowel [a]. Similarly, when a and o occur in such an unstressed position after y or e or before y, e or и they also represent unstressed [a] even if they are not in the position immediately before the stress.

[ъ] does not occur in the positions described above. It occurs in unstressed syllables after the stressed syllable and also in unstressed syllables before the stressed syllable, provided they are not those 'reserved' for unstressed [a].

In positions *after* the stressed syllable, [ъ] may be represented by the letter я (as well as a and o). In such cases the letter я signifies [ъ] preceded either by [й] or a soft consonant.[1]

EXERCISE 15. Practise the following words: дома [дамá] *houses*, дома [дóмъ] *at home*, вода [вадá] *water*, одного [аднавó] *one (g.sg.m.*), от одного [атъднавó] *from one*, у одного [уаднавó] *at one*, на одно [нааднó] *on one*, адвокат [адвакáт] *advocate*, много [мнóгъ] *many*, садовод [съдавóт] *horticulturist*, сообразовал [саабрързавáл] *adapted*, нагая [нагáйъ] *naked (f.*), босая [басáйъ] *barefoot (f.*), зная [знáйъ] *knowing*, надобная [нáдъбнъйъ] *necessary (f.*), соучаствовал [саучáсвъвъл] *participated*.

[1] The letter я in syllables *before* the stressed syllable signifies the vowel [ь], preceded by [й] or a soft consonant (see Chapter 8). Many Russians pronounce final e in the nom. sg. neuter of nouns and adjectives as [ъ], while others pronounce [ь] here, e.g. надобное [нáдъбнъйъ], [нáдъбнъйь], море [мóр'ъ], [мóр'ь] *sea*. The modern tendency seems to be towards [ь].

3

FIVE VOWELS

[и]

THE nearest RP 'equivalent' to Russian [и] is the -ea- in *cease*. There are, however, significant differences which must be carefully observed. Firstly, Russian [и] is a much closer sound than is the -ea- in *cease*; i.e. the front of the tongue is nearer the hard palate.

EXERCISE 16. Pronounce the English word *yield*. Now pronounce it without the final two consonants: *yie*... Now begin to pronounce this syllable but, instead of going on from the *y*- into the following vowel carry on the *y* itself as a vowel. The result should be very like the Russian [и], possibly with a slight *y*- in front of it. If this is the case, try to pronounce this vowel without the slight *y*- in front of it.

In RP and GA the -ea- in *cease* is often slightly like a diphthong, beginning with a vowel like that in *bit* before becoming 'properly' -ea-. Any such tendency to make [и] like a diphthong must be avoided.

EXERCISE 17. Pronounce the vowel learnt in the preceding exercise, trying to make sure that the proper [и]-quality is reached at once and is not preceded by some other vowel-sound. Prolong the vowel [и] and see that there is no change in its quality. Observe the mouth in a mirror and make sure that, once the vowel has been formed, there is no movement of the lips or the lower jaw.

The RP and GA -ea- sound is nearly always rather prolonged. Compare the words *bit* and *beat*, for example: apart from a clear difference in the quality of the vowels there is also a very clear difference in length. The -ea- in *beat* may be said to be intrinsically long, while the -i- in *bit* may be said to be intrinsically short. Differences of vowel-length occur in Russian, too, but these differences are purely the result of the phonetic circumstances, they are 'accidental'. Stressed vowels, for instance, are usually longer than unstressed vowels in Russian, though even this does not hold for all positions in which vowels occur. There is, therefore, no such thing in Russian as an intrinsic difference between long and short vowels. All vowels should be thought of as being the same length—*short*—and then any differences in length will arise automatically if the habits of Russian pronunciation are learnt properly. Russian [и], therefore, should not be thought of as long as RP and GA -*ea*- and indeed should not usually *sound* as long as -*ea*-.

EXERCISE 18. Pronounce the sound already practised in Exercises 9 and 10, concentrating on making it as short as possible. (The shorter the sound is kept the less likely it is to tend towards a slight diphthongisation.)

If all the above points are carefully observed, learnt and thoroughly practised, a considerable difference will be heard between RP *eager*[1] and Russian иго [и́гъ] *yoke*.

Scots speakers should have no trouble at all in pronouncing Russian [и], since the majority of them have a vowel in, for example, *beat* which for all practical purposes is identical with Russian [и].

The sound [и] in Russian is always represented by the letter и.

EXERCISE 19. Practise the following words: чин [чин] *rank*, иго [и́гъ] *yoke*, ива [и́въ] *willow*, ибо [и́бъ] *for*, инок [и́нък] *monk*, чисто [чи́стъ] *cleanly*, иск [иск] *law-suit*, чьи [чйи] *whose (n.pl.)*.

Unstressed [и] is discussed in Chapter 8.

[y]

The nearest RP and GA sound to the Russian [y] is that which is most often represented in spelling by *oo*, as in *soon*. The Russian sound, however, is closer than the English sound, i.e. the back of the tongue is raised higher and is thus nearer to the soft palate. The English *oo*-sound, when pronounced carefully, is made with the lips rounded or pursed, as is Russian [y]. Frequently, however, the sound is made in English with the lips rather lax, so that the rounded shape is not at all apparent. This can happen, to a smaller extent, in Russian but if the student practises the sound with the lips well rounded he is more likely to achieve the correct Russian sound.

EXERCISE 20. Say *soon*, observing the lips in a mirror. Repeat the word, making sure that the lips are well rounded. Say the vowel in *soon* on its own, still making sure that the lips are well rounded and that, no matter how long the sound is prolonged, the lips do not alter their shape at all.

---

[1] In GA and Scots this word ends with an *r*-sound.

C

The RP and GA *oo* is a long sound; the Russian [y] is short. RP and GA speakers sometimes have a tendency to diphthongise the vowel, starting with something like the vowel in *put* before going on to the vowel in *soon*. Any such tendency to diphthongisation is quite wrong for the Russian sound [y].

Scots speakers do not usually have the tendency to make the *oo* in *soon* into a slight diphthong but the vowel they have here is not as far back in the mouth as is the corresponding RP vowel: the lips are rounded but a part of the tongue much nearer the front is raised. Scots speakers should then try one or both of the following methods: (*a*) take the vowel in their pronunciation of *cloak* and, keeping the tongue in the back position (as it is for this vowel), try to pronounce the -*oo*- of *soon*; (*b*) try to make the -*oo*- of *soon* more like a *w*, the result aimed at being not *w* followed by *oo* but a single, back vowel. It also helps to keep the lips well pursed in aiming at Russian [y].

Russian [y] is represented in spelling either by the letter у or by the letter ю. In the latter case the letter ю represents the sound [y] preceded by a soft consonant or by [й].

EXERCISE 21. Practise the following words: ум [ум] *mind*, ну [ну] *well!*, вуз[1] [вус] *higher educational institution*, дума [дýмъ] *thought*, юг [йук] *south*, суп [суп] *soup*, дуб [дуп] *oak*, зуб [зуп] *tooth*.

Unstressed [y] is very like the vowel in RP and GA *pull*. The tongue is not raised as high as in the pronunciation of stressed [y] and the point of highest arching of the tongue is somewhat further forward. A 'relaxed' pronunciation of the [y] described in the preceding paragraphs should result in the formation of an adequate unstressed [y]. Scots speakers use a vowel in the word *pull* which is not as far back as the vowel heard in the English pronunciation of this word and is in fact identical with the vowel they use in *pool*. They will have to start by learning to pronounce stressed [y] properly and then learn to pronounce this in a relaxed manner to arrive at unstressed [y]. At all costs they must avoid using their native vowel (as in *pull*, *pool*) for Russian [y] (stressed or unstressed).

Unstressed [y] is represented in spelling, like stressed [y], by у or ю, the latter symbol representing [y] preceded by [й] or by a soft consonant.

[1] Abbreviation of высшее учебное заведение.

Exercise 22. Practise the following words: ума [умá] *mind* (*g.sg.*), чума [чумá] *plague*, думу [дýму] *thought* (*a.sg.*), знаю [знáйу] *I know*, губа [губá] *lip*, игу [úгу] *yoke* (*d.sg.*), иву [úву] *willow* (*a.sg.*), суда [судá] *court of law* (*g.sg.*), югозапад [йугазáпът][1] *south-west*.

[ə]

The Russian vowel [ə], which occurs only in stressed syllables, is more open than the *e* in English *get*, *net*, etc., i.e. the front of the tongue is further away from the hard palate. It is nearly as open as the vowel heard in English *cat*, *mat*, etc. Students may, therefore, find it convenient to aim at a vowel intermediate between the vowel in *get* and the vowel in *cat*. Alternatively, RP and GA speakers may use as an adequate substitute for [ə] the vowel which occurs at the beginning of the word written *air*.

In RP the word *air* is pronounced as a diphthong, the final point being very close to the Russian vowel [ъ]. Russian [ə] itself is slightly diphthongal, ending in a slight suggestion of [ъ], so that a very fine transcription might be [əᵇ]. This second element, however, is very short and must certainly not be exaggerated. It is better to omit it than to have it sound like a full vowel forming another syllable. Before certain sounds, e.g. [ш], [ж], [р], the [ъ]-element is in any case extremely short or is omitted altogether.

In GA the word *air* consists of a vowel very similar to Russian [ə], followed, however, by an *r*-sound. Such speakers, having isolated the vowel in *air* should then make it slightly diphthongal [əᵇ] but, as was emphasised in the preceding paragraph, the [ъ]-element must not be exaggerated.

Scots speakers pronounce *air* somewhat differently: the vowel is close to that in their pronunciation of *bay* and, as in GA, is followed by an *r*-sound. The word *air* is not, therefore, such a good starting-point for [ə] as it is for RP and GA speakers. The vowel in Scots *pearl*, however, is close to Russian [ə] and, if isolated, can be used as an adequate substitute for Russian [ə], with the addition of the very slight final [ъ]-element.

[ə] is represented in spelling by the letter э—usually only at the beginning of a word—and, more commonly by the letter e. In the latter case [ə] is preceded by [й], a soft consonant or one of the hard consonants [ц], [ш] or [ж].

---

[1] Or [йу̐гъ-зáпът] with a secondary stress (see Chapter 11).

EXERCISE 23. Practise the following words: это [э́тъ] *this, that,*
эра [э́ръ] *era,* ест [йэ́ст] *eats,* чек [чэк] *cheque,* шест [шэст] *pole,*
жест [жэст] *gesture,* ценз [цэнс] *qualification,* цеп [цэп] *flail.*

[o]

Russian [o] is a back vowel, with lip-rounding, similar to the
vowel in RP *thaw, thought,* etc. There are two main differences
between the RP vowel and Russian [o]: the Russian vowel, like
all Russian vowels, is not intrinsically long, whereas the RP vowel,
like some but not all RP vowels, is intrinsically long, and the
Russian vowel is not as open as the RP vowel, i.e. the back of the
tongue is slightly higher, slightly nearer the soft palate.

Some RP speakers, however, use a vowel in words such as the
ones quoted above which is more close than that used perhaps by
the majority and which is, in fact, very near to Russian [o]. Such
speakers usually have the lips more rounded than those who use
a more open vowel in *thaw,* etc. Russian [o] too is accompanied
by fairly strong lip-rounding. In aiming at Russian [o], therefore,
RP speakers should have the lips well rounded.

EXERCISE 24. Pronounce the word *caught,* making the vowel as
short as in the word *cot.* If *caught* then sounds not too unlike *cot,*
the probability is that you use a fairly open vowel in *caught.* You
will have to make this vowel more close, using more lip-rounding,
in order to arrive at a satisfactory starting-point for Russian [o].
If on the other hand *caught* pronounced with the vowel short
sounds quite unlike *cot,* the probability is that you already have
a good starting-point for Russian [o].

GA and Scots speakers usually have a very open vowel in *thaw*
and *thought* and will, therefore, have to effect a good deal more
'closing' of this vowel to approach [o]. They may also try to aim
at a vowel intermediate between that in *home* and that in *thaw.*
Strong lip-rounding will help in reaching the right quality.

Russian [o] also differs from the similar vowels used by speakers
of various types of English in that it is slightly diphthongal: it
starts as [o] and ends with a very slight suggestion of the vowel [ъ],
thus [oᵇ].[1] This final element is very brief and is on no account to
be exaggerated into another syllable.

---

[1] This applies only when [o] is not followed by a soft consonant. When
it is followed by a soft consonant, [o] ends with a very slight suggestion of
the vowel [ь] or unstressed [и]. (See Chapter 5, p. 37, footnote 2.)

[o] occurs in stressed syllables and also occasionally in syllables with secondary stress and in a few monosyllabic unstressed words.[1]

The vowel [o] is represented in spelling by the letters o and e. In the latter case (when the letter e is sometimes provided with a diaeresis: ё) the vowel [o] is preceded by [й], by a soft consonant or by [ш] or [ж].

EXERCISE 25. Practise the following words: сон [сон] *sleep*, дом [дом] *house*, нов [ноф] *new*, мозг [моск] *brain*, шов [шоф] *seam*, еж [йош] *hedgehog*, объем [абйóм] *volume*, шелк [шолк] *silk*, жен [жон] *wives* (*g.pl.*).

[ы]

Russian [ы] is a very close vowel: the tongue is lifted as near to the palate as in the pronunciation of [и] and [у] but the point of the tongue which is raised highest is neither at the front (as in the case of [и]) nor at the back (as in the case of [у]). It is the middle of the tongue which is raised to the middle of the palate: [ы] is a close, 'central' vowel.

Many students experience considerable difficulty in making this sound and yet, once a student has become used to the 'feel' of various vowels, i.e. to the various positions of the lips and tongue and, if he is not a good mimic, to the technique of adapting his English vowels to Russian ones, he should not in fact be put to too much trouble in obtaining at least a good approximation to [ы].

[ы] strikes the English-speaking student as being like the *i* in *sin* but somewhat 'cloudy', 'obscure'. [ы] is, in fact, a sound of the *i*-type but, whereas *i* is formed with the front of the tongue raised, [ы]—as was explained above—is formed with the middle of the tongue raised.

EXERCISE 26. Try to pronounce the word *sin* with the middle of the tongue raised up towards the middle of the hard palate. The tip of the tongue does not, of course, enter into the formation of the vowel: it will be approaching the teeth-ridge ready to make the contact for *n*. The word *sin*, pronounced thus, will be—apart from the difference in the articulation of *n* between Russian and English —a very fair approximation to the Russian word сын [сын] *son*.

After [б], [п], [м], [в] and [ф] Russian [ы] sounds even more 'cloudy' or 'obscure'. This is because it is pronounced even further

---

[1] See Chapter 11.

back in the mouth, with the back of the tongue raised at a point nearer to that for [y].

EXERCISE 27 (for RP and GA speakers). Say the English word *book*. Observe in a mirror that, with careful pronunciation, the lips are rounded in enunciating this word. Now say the word again *with the lips spread*, as if you were saying *beak*, but with the tongue trying to make the -*oo*- sound. If you find this difficult, practise at first with the little finger of each hand in the corners of the mouth pulling the lips into a spread position while you say *book*. The result should be a fair approximation to the Russian word бык [бык] *bull*. If the word still sounds like *book*, you have probably not spread your lips properly.

If the student is unable to acquire the truly central [ы] by means of Exercise 26, he should start with Exercise 27 and, having acquired and fully practised the back variety of [ы], then try to make this sound further forward in the mouth (without, of course, reaching the [и] position) in order to acquire the central [ы].

It was pointed out above in the section on Russian [y] that Scots speakers do not have the RP vowel which occurs in such words as *book* and *pull* and that they have instead a vowel which is pronounced with the lips rounded but the middle of the tongue, not the back, raised. If they pronounce the word *soon* with the lips spread they will have a fair approximation to the Russian word сын [сын] *son*.

Another method which students may try is to say the Russian vowel [ъ] with the lips spread. The resultant vowel will be like an unstressed [ы]. It then remains to make this vowel with the middle of the tongue nearer the hard palate in order to obtain something like the stressed Russian [ы] in [сын].

Russian [ы] is short. The student should take care not to make [ы] a long vowel.

[ы] is represented in spelling by the letter ы *and also by the letter* и (when this occurs after the letters ш, ж or ц, or as the first letter in a word preceded by a preposition ending in any hard consonant).

Unstressed [ы] has, to the ears of English-speaking students, a similar 'cloudy' or 'obscure' quality to that of stressed [ы]. The tongue is raised in the middle, as for stressed [ы], but not as high as for the latter vowel. Stressed [ы] pronounced in a 'relaxed' manner and with not much lip-spreading will give the quality of unstressed [ы]. Unstressed [ы] is represented in spelling in the same way as stressed [ы].

EXERCISE 28. Practise the following words: сын [сын] *son*, вы [вы] *you*, дым [дым] *smoke*, мы [мы] *we*, мыс [мыс] *cape, headland*, бык [бык] *bull*, цинк [цынк] *zinc*, овцы [афцы́] *sheep* (*g.sg.*), шил [шыл] *sewed*, жил [жыл] *lived*; (unstressed [ы]): сынок [сынóк] *little son*, жила [жылá] *lived* (*f.*), овцы [óфцы] *sheep* (*pl.*), думы [дýмы] *thoughts*, губы [гýбы] *lips*, с ивы [сы́вы] *from the willow*, от Ивана [атывáнъ] *from John*.

4

SIX CONSONANTS

(a) [п], [т], [к]

ALTHOUGH several words used as examples in previous chapters have involved the consonants [п], [т], [к] a description of these consonants has been reserved until this chapter for a reason which will become apparent below.

[п] is, apart from one important particular, identical with the consonant at the beginning of such English words as *pat, put, pot*, etc. [к], one important particular again being excepted, is identical with the consonant at the beginning of such English words as *cat, cut, coat*, etc.

Russian [т] is similar to the *t* in such English words as *tack, took*, etc. but, as far as the point of articulation is concerned, differs from *t* in the same way that [д] differs from *d*, i.e. it is *dental*, formed with the tip of the tongue in the angle of the upper teeth and gums and not with the tip of the tongue against the teeth-ridge. The student may find it useful to perform an exercise similar to that suggested for [д] by marking in a reading passage all the occurrences of [т] in order to draw his attention to the fact that [т] is dental. He should repeat this with various passages until he is confident that he makes [т] dental without a conscious effort of memory.

The 'important particular' in which [п] and [к] differ from the corresponding English sounds concerns [т] also. When the corresponding English consonants occur immediately before a stressed vowel they are usually slightly 'aspirated'.[1] This means that a faint puff of air is emitted between the consonant and the following vowel.

EXERCISE 29. Hold the back of the hand at a distance of about four inches from the mouth and say the syllable *ba* and then *pa*. You should—if you aspirate the *p* in *pa*—feel a slight puff of air against the back of the hand which is not felt when you say *ba*.

---

[1] This does not usually happen when they occur before unstressed consonants.

You may also notice that the vowel in *pa* begins with a somewhat 'breathy' quality. This is because the vowel is not voiced throughout: it begins as a 'voiceless' vowel. Repeat the exercise with *ga*, *ka* and *da*, *ta*. The puff of air should still be fairly palpable with *ta* but may escape your notice when you pronounce *ka*, though in the latter case the 'breathy' quality of the vowel should still be fairly evident. You may find it necessary to bring the hand close up to the mouth in order to detect the aspiration of *k* in *ka*. An alternative way of performing this exercise is to hold a lighted match about four inches from the mouth while saying the syllables given above. With *ba*, *ga* and *da* the flame should remain steady (though it may flicker slightly *after* you have finished each syllable), whereas with *pa*, *ka*, *ba* the flame will probably be found to flicker slightly a fraction of a second after you have made the consonants. The flickering is caused by the puff of air emitted from the mouth in the aspiration of the consonants.

The Russian consonants [п], [т], [к] are not aspirated.[1] An aspirated [т] before a vowel may sound to a Russian like a soft [т'] or even like [ц], while an aspirated [к] may sound to a Russian like a sequence of [к] and the Russian consonant [x] (see next section). It is important, therefore, that the student should learn to avoid aspiration of [п], [т], [к], though usually it is not very easy for English speakers to avoid such aspiration.

Exercise 30. Try to make consonants which are, respectively, intermediate between [п] and [б], [т] and [д], [к] and [г], i.e. combine the voicelessness of [п], [т], [к] and the non-aspiration of [б], [д], [г]. Other methods you may try are as follows: hold the breath for a moment before saying, for example, [па], [та] and [ка] or try to say these syllables with a slightly constricted throat, i.e. with the throat muscles tightened. Yet another method is to take advantage of the fact that in English the corresponding consonants are not normally aspirated before unstressed vowels, or are only very slightly aspirated in this position.[2] Take such vocables as [апа], [ата], [ака], pronouncing them with a slight stress on the first vowel, and then try to isolate the second syllable, beginning in each case with an unaspirated consonant. Another

---

[1] Except when they occur at the end of a word before a pause: the emission of a slight puff of air here as the consonants are released is not wrong but the student would be well advised to keep it to a minimum.

[2] GA speakers should *not* use this method for [т].

method is to take advantage of the fact that after *s* English *p*, *t*, *k* are only very slightly aspirated, if at all. Take such words as *span*, *stand* and *scan* (where *k* is represented by *c*) and try to isolate the almost or entirely unaspirated *p*, *t*, *k* in these words or shorten the initial *s* until it disappears.

[п] is represented in spelling by the letter п and also by б (at the end of a word and before a letter representing a voiceless consonant).

[т] is represented in spelling by the letter т and also by д (at the end of a word and before a letter representing a voiceless consonant).

[к] is represented in spelling by the letter к and also by г (at the end of a word and before a letter representing a voiceless consonant).[1]

EXERCISE 31. Practise the following words: (i) почва [по́чвъ] *soil*, упадок [упа́дък] *decline*, способ [спо́съп] *means*, пот [пот] *sweat*, юбка [йу́пкъ] *skirt*, зуб [зуп] *tooth*; (ii) тот [тот] *that*, тут [тут] *here*, потом [пато́м] *then*, стан [стан] *stature*, отпуск [о́тпуск] *leave*, год [гот] *year*; (iii) ком [ком] *clod*, кот [кот] *tom-cat*, куча [ку́чъ] *heap*, стакан [стака́н] *glass*, кадка [ка́ткъ] *tub*, юг [йук] *south*.

(*b*)   [ш], [ж], [х]
[ш]

The nearest English sound to Russian [ш] is that commonly represented by *sh* in English spelling (as in *shop*). English *sh*, however, sounds somewhat 'sharper' than Russian [ш]—it has, in fact, a higher pitch. This higher pitch of English *sh* is a result of the fact that *sh* is made with more of the front of the tongue against the hard palate.

EXERCISE 32. Isolate the sound represented by *sh* in *shop* and prolong it—*shhhh!* Note that the tip of the tongue is just about on the teeth-ridge (without making a firm contact) and that the front of the tongue is curved up or lifted up very close to the hard palate. You will also notice that there is quite a firm contact between the sides of the tongue and the inside of the upper gums and teeth. Now move the tip of the tongue very slightly higher up, just behind the teeth-ridge, where it begins to rise up into the roof of the mouth. Let the tongue be somewhat more relaxed, so that the sides are not pressing so firmly against the upper gums.

[1] For the value of г in certain words see Chapter 10.

Now say *shhhh!* again. Repeat with the lips somewhat more protruded. The resultant sound should be a close approximation to Russian [ш].

Russian [ш] is represented in spelling by the letter ш, by the letter ж (at the end of a word and also before [ф], [с], [ц], [т], [к], [ш] if and when these combinations occur) and by с and з (before ш).[1] The so-called 'soft sign'—ь—sometimes occurs after ш and ж and, though the function of this sign is usually to indicate that the preceding consonant is 'soft', it has no effect on the value of the symbols ш and ж.

EXERCISE 33. Practise the following words: шаг [шак] *step*, шум [шум] *noise*, ушиб [ушып] *injury*, вошь [вош] *louse*, ножка [нóшкъ] *foot*, пассаж [пасáш] *passage*, сшиб [шшып] *knocked down*, еж [йош] *hedgehog*, из шубы [ишшýбы] *out of the fur-coat*, ложь [лош] *lie*.

[ж]

The nearest English sound to Russian [ж] is that represented by *s* in *measure, leisure* or by *g* in *rouge*. The English sound differs from Russian [ж] in just the same way that English *sh* differs from Russian [ш] (see preceding section). The student should either isolate the sound represented by *s* in *measure* and adapt it to the Russian [ж] in the same way that he adapted *sh* to [ш], or, having learnt [ш], make it voiced, thus producing [ж]. [ж] must be voiced throughout.

[ж] is represented in spelling by the letter ж, by ш (if and when this letter occurs before a letter representing [б], [б'], [д], [г], [г'], [з], [з'] or [ж]) and by с and з (before [ж]).[2]

EXERCISE 34. Practise the following words: жаба [жáбъ] *toad*, жук [жук] *beetle*, жив [жыф] *alive*, жест [жэст] *gesture*, вожак [важáк] *leader*, обжег [абжóк] *scorched*, сжег [жжок] *burnt up*, с жажды [жжáжды] *from thirst*, изжога [ижжóгъ] *heartburn*.

[x]

There is no sound in RP and GA which can be said to be near Russian [x]. Scots, however, has a very similar sound—heard at the end of the word *loch*, for example—though there is much less noise with Russian [x], only a very slight friction being heard.

[1] In a few words [ш] is represented by ч. See Chapter 10.
[2] For the value of ж in such words as дождь, дождя, etc., see Chapter 10.

Scots students and those who can imitate the *ch* in *loch* should use this sound as a basis for [x], relaxing the articulation so that hardly any friction is heard.

For others it will be of help to know that Russian [x] is formed in the same place and almost in the same manner as English *k* and Russian [к], i.e. with the back of the tongue against the soft palate. However, instead of being pressed against the soft palate, so that the stream of air issuing from the lungs is momentarily stopped, the back of the tongue is almost touching the soft palate, so that the air stream passes between the tongue and soft palate, producing friction.

EXERCISE 35. Say the English sound *k*. Now put the tongue in the position for *k* and push the air stream against it for a while before releasing the tongue to make the 'explosion' of *k*. You should be able to sense the contact of tongue and soft palate. Do this again, but this time release the tongue slowly or, in rather inaccurate terms, make a 'slow *k*'. You will probably find that there is now a somewhat indistinct *k* followed by a harsh, scraping noise, almost like the sound made when clearing phlegm from the back of the mouth. Alternatively, make a 'forceful' *k*, i.e. 'eject' the sound from the back of the mouth, as it were. You may again find that the *k* is followed by a harsh, scraping noise. Now try to produce this scraping noise without the preceding *k*. The resultant sound is a variety of [x]. For Russian [x] the friction and the resultant scraping noise must be reduced to a minimum. (It is better to use an ordinary English *h* than to have too much friction in Russian [x]).

Russian [x] is represented in spelling by the letter x.[1]

EXERCISE 36. Practise the following words: хата [ха́тъ] *hut*, хочу [хачу́] *I want*, худо [ху́дъ] *evil*, хвост [хвост] *tail*, мох [мох] *moss*, дух [дух] *spirit*, сухо [су́хъ] *drily*, запах [за́пъх] *smell*, пахота [па́хътъ] *tillage*, махну [махну́] *I will wave*, духовка [духо́фкъ] *oven*, Пасха [па́схъ] *Easter*, мха [мха] *moss* (*g.sg.*).

---

[1] For г representing [x] in certain words, see Chapter 10.

5

SOFT CONSONANTS

(a) INTRODUCTORY

ALL the consonants described so far are 'hard' consonants, with the exception of [ч] (which was said to be a 'soft' consonant) and [й] (which is also a 'soft' consonant, though attention has not been called to this, since it presents no difficulties). 'Hard' and 'soft' in this context are, of course, metaphorical terms and have nothing to do with tactile concepts of hardness and softness. Broadly speaking, a soft consonant is one in the formation of which some part or other of the tongue is brought nearer the hard palate than in the formation of the corresponding hard consonant. Acoustically, the effect of softening is a raising of the pitch.

In the formation of some of the hard consonants described in preceding chapters the tongue is not used at all ([п], [б], [м], [ф], [в]), whereas in the formation of the other consonants described above some part of the tongue is used—tip, front or back. From this point of view, soft consonants may be divided into two groups: (a) those in which the 'normal' or hard articulation of the consonant is preserved, the further articulation of softening being added, and (b) those in which the 'normal' or hard articulation is modified. The first group comprises [п'], [б'], [м'], [ф'], [в'] (soft [п], [б], etc.). The second group comprises [т'], [д'], [н'], [с'], [з'], [л'], [р'], [ш'], [ж'], [к'], [г'], [х'] (soft [т], [д], [н], [с], etc.). [ч], which was described in Chapter 2, is a soft consonant because, in forming it, the tongue and palate are used in a way similar to that in which they are used in the formation of other soft consonants in the second group. It has no hard counterpart in Russian.

There is *no* soft counterpart to [ц], so that, even when the letter ц is followed by a vowel letter which normally indicates softening of the preceding consonant, ц still represents hard [ц], e.g. цех [цэх] *workshop*. The soft sign (ь) and vowel letters which normally indicate softening have no effect on the value of the letters ш and ж, thus шест [шэст] *pole*, жест [жэст] *gesture*, with hard [ш] and [ж].

35

Soft [ш'] and [ж'] do occur, however, and the way in which they are indicated will be described in Chapter 7.

Softness of most consonants is indicated in spelling by the soft sign (ь) or by one of the special vowel letters и, е, я, ю. The soft sign or special vowel letter follows the letter for the consonant which is soft: сила [с'и́лъ] *strength*, путь [пут'] *path*, тяга [т'а́гъ] *draught*, etc. The letter ч always indicates a soft consonant so that one might expect to find after it only the special vowel letters and ь, *or* only the ordinary vowel letters (since the softness of [ч] is, so to speak, included in the letter ч itself).[1] The conventions of Russian spelling, however, are чи, че, чо and чу. One does not find чы, чэ, чя or чю. The letter ч followed by the soft sign is found, frequently in the infinitive, e.g. толо́чь [тало́ч] *to pound*, and also in some other forms, e.g. чье *whose*. In the latter case the function of the soft sign is to indicate the presence of the consonant [й] between the soft consonant [ч] and the following vowel: чье [чйо] (see Chapter 10).

When two or more consonant letters occur together and the last one represents a soft consonant then the preceding ones may also represent soft consonants. This phenomenon is discussed in Chapter 9, section (*c*).

(*b*) EIGHT SOFT CONSONANTS

(i) [п'], [б'], [м'], [ф'], [в']

These five soft consonants are formed with the lips in exactly the same position as for their hard counterparts but at the same time the tongue is placed in the position for Russian [и]. For a brief moment after the consonant has been formed (and released) the tongue is kept in this position and then the following vowel is made. The result of this is that there appears between the consonant and the following vowel a very short sound like Russian [й] or English *y* (as in *yet*). It must be emphasised that this intervening sound or 'glide' is very brief and that it must on no account be exaggerated or prolonged. Soft [п'] for example, is like the '*py*' sound in English *pure* but the [й] element is much less obvious. This is particularly so when the vowel following [п'], [б'], [м'], [ф'], [в'] is [и].

---

[1] ч also indicates [ш'] and [ш] in certain circumstances. See Chapters 6 and 10.

Students who find difficulty in placing the tongue in the [и] position while pronouncing the above consonants should try the following exercise, which is also useful for obtaining the very slight glide before [и].

EXERCISE 37. Practise the vocables [ип'и], [иб'и], [им'и], [иф'и], [ив'и], keeping the tongue in the [и] position *throughout* and gradually reducing the initial vowel until it disappears.

At the end of a word the glide due to the softening will be heard very briefly after the consonant. Since [б'] and [в'] do not occur at the end of a word, being replaced by [п'] and [ф'] respectively, the glide after these consonants will be voiceless, as are [п'] and [ф']. It is not difficult to make this voiceless glide: if one goes through the procedure for making [п'] and [ф'] correctly, keeping the voice silent, the voiceless glide will arise of its own accord.

[м'], like [м], remains voiced at the end of a word[1] but the glide is usually hardly audible or even entirely inaudible, though the presence of soft [м'] may be revealed by the quality of the preceding vowel. Thus, семь [с'ем'] *seven* may have no audible softness of the [м] but it has the vowel [e] *which occurs only in front of soft consonants.*

The soft consonants [п'], [б'], [м'], [ф'], [в'] are represented in spelling by the same letters that represent their hard counterparts, followed of course by one of the letters и, е, я, ю or ь, or by certain other soft consonants (see Chapter 9).

EXERCISE 38. Practise the following words: пиво [п'íвъ] *beer*, пена [п'э́нъ] *foam*, пес [п'ос] *dog*, пятка [п'а́ткъ] *heel*; бинт [б'инт] *bandage*, бес [б'эс] *demon*, бюст [б'уст] *bust*; фикция [ф'и́кцыйъ] *fiction*, феска [ф'эскъ] *fez*, Федор [ф'о́дър] *Theodore*; вид [в'ит] *view*, век [в'эк] *age*, вязка [в'а́скъ] *bundle*; миг [м'ик] *moment*, место [м'эстъ] *place*, мед [м'от] *honey*, мясо [м'а́съ] *meat*; топь [топ']² *swamp*, насыпь [на́сып'] *embankment*, зыбь [зып'] *swell*, обувь [о́буф']² *footwear*, вновь [вноф']² *anew*.

---

[1] [м] is, however, voiceless on the very rare occasions when it occurs at the end of a word and is preceded by a voiceless consonant, e.g. драхм [драхм] *drachma* (*g.pl.*). A voiceless [м] consists simply of air issuing through the nose while the lips are closed.

[2] Between [o], [y] or [a] and a following soft consonant there is a slight glide, rather like a very short [ь] or unstressed [и], or English *i* (as in *bits*). This glide must not be so exaggerated that the result is a diphthong like [ой], [уй] or [ай].

(ii)   [к'], [г'], [x']

These three soft consonants are of the second type of soft consonant discussed at the beginning of this chapter, i.e. softening has the effect of altering the point of articulation as compared with the point of articulation of the hard counterparts. Hard [к], [г], [x] are formed by a contact (or near-contact, in the case of [x]) between the back of the tongue and the soft palate, whereas for [к'], [г'], [x'] the contact (or near-contact, in the case of [x']) is further forward in the mouth. Again, the result of this is a very short [й]-type sound between the consonant and the following vowel, a sound which will be less in evidence when the following vowel is [и] and which, in any case, is usually less evident than the [й]-type sound, or glide, which follows [п'], [б'], etc.

The student who is unable to produce [к'], [г'], [x'] by following the description given above should try one or both of the following exercises.

EXERCISE 39. Take the '*ky*' sound in the word *cube* and try, so to speak, to merge '*ky*' into one sound to produce [к']. Try the same procedure with the '*gy*' sound in *argue*, in order to produce [г']

EXERCISE 40. Say the words *keel* and *cool* and keep on saying them until you can feel that the *k* in *keel* is made at a point slightly further forward in the mouth than is the *k* (represented by the letter *c*) in *cool*. When you have done this to your satisfaction, try saying the word *keel* with the *k* even further forward in the mouth. Try the same procedure with *geese* and *goose*.

It may help in making [к'] and [г'] to think of them as 'mixtures' of or sounds intermediate between *k* and *ch*, *g* and *j* (as in *jig*) respectively. On no account, however, should [к'] and [г'] be made so far forward in the mouth that they become sounds of the *ch* and *j* types: they should always be clearly like sounds of the *k* and *g* types.

[к'] and [г'] are represented in spelling by the letters which represent [к] and [г] respectively (see above), followed however by one of the vowel letters и or e.[1] The adjective endings -кий and -гий are pronounced by some Russians as [-к'и] and [-г'и], by others as [-къй] and [-гъй].

---

[1] Exceptions to this are the personal names Лукьян [лук'йáн], Лукьянов [лук'йáнъф], the place-name Кяхта [к'áхтъ] and one or two nouns, such as маникюр [мън'ик'ýр] *manicure*.

The sound [x'] stands in the same relationship to [x] as does [к'] to [к]. One might also say that [x'] stands in the same relationship to [к'] as does [x] to [к]. There are thus two ways of reaching [x']: (i) the articulation of [x] can be made further forward in the mouth, so as to produce [x']—just as the articulation of [к] is brought forward so as to produce [к']: or (ii) having learnt [к'] one can then apply to it the techniques described in Chapter 4 to produce [x] from [к]; when these techniques are applied to [к'] the result will be at least a close approximation to [x'].

Some English speakers pronounce the words *hue, hew, Hugh* with an initial sound very like [x'], instead of *h*. Such a sound will make a very acceptable [x'].

[x'], like [x], must not be made with a harsh, rasping noise.

[x'] is represented in spelling by the letter x followed by и or e. It is also represented by г in some words (Chapter 10).

The adjective ending -хий is pronounced by some Russians as [-x'и], by others as [-хъй] (with hard [x]).

EXERCISE 41. Practise the following words: кипа [к'ипъ] *stack,* кисточка [к'истъчкъ] *shaving-brush,* кем [к'эм] *by whom,* в руке [врук'э] *in the hand,* ткешь [тк'ош] *you weave,* ткет [тк'от] *he weaves,* гипс [г'ипс] *plaster-of-paris,* шаги [шаг'и] *steps,* гемма [г'эммъ] *gem,* богема [баг'эмъ] *bohemianism,* хина [х'инъ] *Peruvian bark,* хижина [х'ижынъ] *hut,* сухим [сух'им] *dry (inst.sg.m.),* в дохе [вдах'э] *in a fur coat.*

6

SEVEN SOFT CONSONANTS

THE last section of the preceding chapter described three soft consonants of the second type, in which the softening modifies the point and manner of articulation. The soft consonants in this chapter are of this second type.

[c'] AND [ʒ']

The consonants [c'] and [ʒ'] are formed with the tongue-tip against the teeth-ridge and at the same time the front of the tongue is raised close to the hard palate as if one were trying to pronounce [и] simultaneously with [c] or [ʒ]. The parts of the tongue used in the formation of these soft consonants are then released in smooth succession from the very front backwards, i.e. the tip is lowered and then that part of the front which is close to the hard palate. The result of this is that after the soft [c'] or [ʒ'] a further, very brief sound, a 'glide' in the nature of [й], is heard. When [c'] occurs before a pause the [й]-glide is voiceless. Before the vowel [и] the glide after [c'] or [ʒ'] is hardly noticeable or is entirely absent but the softness of the consonants is maintained. The softness, with or without glide, is manifested by a higher intrinsic pitch, as compared with hard [c] and [ʒ]. On no account must the glide be exaggerated: [c'a] must not sound like [c'иa] or [c'йa] and certainly not like [cйa]. In a very precise transcription [c'a] might be written [c'йa] but such a transcription is not necessary if the student keeps in mind the description given above.

It is possible to form [c'] and [ʒ'] with the tip of the tongue curled down (touching the back of the lower teeth), the very foremost part of the front of the tongue almost touching the teeth-ridge and the remainder of the front of the tongue being raised towards the hard palate. Again, the part which is raised towards the hard palate is lowered last of all, so that the [й]-glide is heard before a following vowel.

In RP and Scots, though not usually in GA, such words as *sue* and *resume* have sounds represented by *s* which are similar to [c'] and [з']. The *s* in *sue* and the *z*-sound in *resume* (represented by *s*) are followed by a sound like the *y* in *youth*. It may help, in trying to produce [с'] and [з'], to pronounce *sue* and *resume* with the *y*-sound fused, as it were, with the preceding consonant. One should always bear in mind, however, that neither [с'] nor [з'], apart from the slight [й]-glide before vowels, ever sounds like a sequence of two consonants.

[с'] is represented in spelling by the letter с (followed by one of the letters и, е, я, ю, ь or one of the sounds [с'], [т'], [н'], [л']),[1] and also by з (when this letter is followed by ь at the end of a word or by ь and a voiceless consonant or when it is followed by a letter representing [с'] or [т']).

[з'] is represented in spelling by the letter з (followed by one of the letters и, е, я, ю, ь or one of the sounds [з'], [д'], [н'], [л']) and also by с (when this letter is followed by ь before [б], [б'], [д], [д'], [г] or [г'] or when it is followed simply by a letter representing [з'] or [д']).

EXERCISE 42. Practise the following words: все [фс'э] *everybody*, все [фс'о] *everything*, сито [с'итъ] *sieve*, косяк [кас'áк] *shoal*, ось [ос'] *axle*, мазь [мас'] *grease*, осью [óс'йу][2] *axle* (*inst.sg.*); зев [з'эф] *pharynx*, газета [газ'этъ] *newspaper*, зимы [з'úмы] *winters*, позем [паз'óм] *manure*, мазью [мáз'йу][2, 3] *grease* (*inst.sg.*), просьба [прóз'бъ] *request*.

[н']

To form [н'] the tongue-tip is placed, as for hard [н], immediately behind the upper teeth (or possibly a little further back), the part of the tongue immediately behind the tip is pressed against the teeth-ridge and the front of the tongue is raised towards the hard palate as if the vowel [и] were being pronounced at the same time. The release of the tongue follows the same sequence as for [с'] and [з'], i.e. tongue-tip first and then the front, so that a glide like the consonant [й] is heard: [н'йa]. The glide must not be exaggerated and it is, in any case, hardly noticeable or entirely absent before [и] and when [н'] is not followed by a vowel.

Like [с'] and [з'], [н'] may also be pronounced with the tip of the tongue curled down (behind the lower teeth) but the softness

---

[1] For the value of с in the reflexive particles -ся and -сь see Chapter 11.

[2] In these words [с'] and [з'] are followed by a clear [й].

[3] See Chapter 5, p. 37, footnote 2.

is maintained by the raising of the front of the tongue towards the hard palate and the [й]-glide is heard in the appropriate circumstances.

English-speaking students who pronounce the word *union* as two syllables have a slightly softened *n* in this word, followed by a sound akin to the *y* in *yet*. Such speakers may find it helpful to approach [н'] by trying to fuse the first *n* in *union* with the following *y*-sound, bearing in mind that, apart from the slight [й]-glide before vowels, [н'] must not sound like a sequence of two consonants.

[н'] is represented in spelling by the letter н (followed by one of the letters и, е, я, ю, ь, ч or щ or one of the sounds [н'], [т'], [д'], [с'] or [з'].

EXERCISE 43. Practise the following words: нет [н'эт] *no*, небо [н'э́бъ] *sky*, небо [н'о́бъ] *palate*, нива [н'и́въ] *cornfield*, конек [кан'о́к] *little horse*, конь [кон'] *horse*, дань [дан'] *tribute*, с данью [здан'йу] *with a tribute*, гончая [го́н'чъйъ] *hound*, вонзить [ван'з'и́т'] *to plunge in*.

[т'] AND [д']

[т'] and [д'] correspond to [т] and [д] in manner of articulation as [н'] corresponds to [н]. The tip of the tongue is placed immediately behind the upper teeth (or possibly a little further back) or it is curled down and rests behind the lower teeth, the part immediately behind the tip is pressed against the teeth-ridge and the front is raised towards the hard palate as if the vowel [и] were being pronounced at the same time. When these consonants are released, the tongue is lowered in such a way that for a fraction of a second a narrow slit is formed between the teeth-ridge and that part of the front of the tongue which has been against it. The air in the mouth which has been held back by the closure formed for [т'] or [д'] issues through this slit, producing a very brief sound akin to [с'] after [т'] and akin to [з'] after [д']. (These 'additional' sounds must be kept very short: [т'] must not sound like [т'с'] nor must [д'] sound like [д'з'].) The front of the tongue is then lowered from the [и] position.

RP speakers pronounce such words as *tune* and *dune* with a *t* and *d*, respectively, followed by a sound like the *y* in *yew*. Such speakers may find it helpful to approach [т'] and [д'] by way of the initial sounds of *tune* and *dune* respectively, trying to fuse the *t* and *d* with the following *y*-sound. Care must be taken, however, not to produce sounds of the type normally written *ch* and *j* respectively (as in *chewed* and *June*). Such sounds are quite wrong for Russian [т'] and [д']. The Russian sounds are, so to speak, intermediate between the initial sounds of *tune, dune* and those of *chewed, June*.

Scots speakers use initially in such words as *tune* and *dune* sounds very like those used by RP speakers. Many GA speakers, however, pronounce these words without a *y*-element after the *t* and *d* or with an element more akin to '*i*' than to '*y*'. Such speakers had better not try to approach [т'] and [д'] by way of the *t* and *d* in *tune* and *dune*.

[т'] is represented in spelling by the letter т (followed by one of the letters и, е, я, ю, ь or ч or one of the sounds [т'], [с'], [ш'], [н'], [л']) and also by д (when this letter is followed by ь at the end of a word or by ь and a voiceless consonant or when it is followed by a letter representing [т'], [с'], [ч] or [ш']).

[д'] is represented in spelling by the letter д (followed by one of the letters и, е, я, ю, ь or one of the sounds [д'], [з'], [н'], [л']) and also by т (when this letter is followed by ь before [б], [б'], or when it is followed simply by a letter representing [д'] or [з']).[1]

EXERCISE 44. Practise the following words[2]: тина [т'инъ] *slime*, тесто [т'эстъ] *dough*, тетка [т'откъ] *auntie*, утюг [ут'ук] *flat-iron*, гость [гос'т'] *guest*, отсюда [ат'с'удъ] *hence*, подтек [пат'т'ок] *bruise*, будь [бут'] *be!*, отчет [ат'чот][3] *account*, костью [кóс'т'йу] *bone (inst.sg.)*; диво [д'ивъ] *marvel*, демон [д'эмън] *demon*, деготь [д'óгът'] *pitch*, гадюка [гад'укъ] *viper*, поддевка [пад'д'óфкъ] (*kind of coat*), подземка [пад'з'эмкъ] *subway*, '*tube*', попадья [пъпад'йá] *priest's wife*, молотьба [мълад'бá] *threshing*.

[1] For the value of the combinations -жд- plus и, е, я, ю or ь see Chapter 10.
[2] A number of words in this exercise have 'double' [т'т'] or [д'д']. In these cases the first [т'] or [д'] is not sounded 'separately', i.e. the tongue is not released and then placed in position for another [т'] or [д']. The tongue is simply held in position for twice the length of time for a single [т'] or [д'], the release, with the concomitant [с'] or [з'] glide, being made only once. In general when [т'] and [д'] are followed by a consonant in the formation of which the tip and/or front of the tongue is used, the [т'] and [д'] are not released separately and the [с'] or [з'] glide is lost.
[3] N.B. [т'], not [т], before [ч]. The tongue is held in position for twice the length of time for single [ч] and no separate release of the [т'] is made. Cp. preceding footnote.

[ш'] AND [ж']

To form the sounds [ш'] and [ж'] the tongue is placed as follows: tip of tongue very close to teeth-ridge, front of tongue high up near the hard palate, sides of tongue pressing against the upper molars. There is no 'hollowing' of the front of the tongue as there is for hard [ш] and [ж].

The sounds [ш'] and [ж'] are respectively more like English *sh* (in *sheep*) and the sound represented by *s* in *measure* than are [ш] and [ж] but they are somewhat softer than these English sounds. That is to say that more of the front of the tongue is raised towards the hard palate in forming [ш'] and [ж'] than in forming the two English sounds just mentioned. The student should practise adapting the two English sounds in this manner.

The sound [ш'] rarely occurs as a single sound but nearly always as one of a pair of consonants. It occurs either in the combination [ш'ш'] (i.e. a long [ш']) or in the combination [ш'ч], in which the closure formed by the front of the tongue against the hard palate at the beginning of the [ч]-element is very weak. These combinations are represented in spelling by the letter щ or by the combinations of letters сч and зч. There are three variant types of pronunciation of these letters: (i) Some speakers pronounce [ш'ш'] for щ, сч or зч; (ii) others pronounce [ш'ч] for щ, сч or зч; (iii) yet others pronounce [ш'ш'] for щ and in many words [ш'ч] for сч or зч. When the letter щ is followed by another consonant letter, e.g. н, it is usual to pronounce simply a single [ш']: сущность [суш'нъс'т'] *essence*, though in a very precise, deliberate style of pronunciation the 'full' value may be given to щ even in this case.

[ж'] is simply the voiced counterpart of [ш'], as [ж] is the voiced counterpart of [ш]. It is of much rarer occurrence than [ш'] though, like [ш'] it never occurs singly: it occurs only in the combination of 'double' [ж'ж'] (i.e. a long [ж']). The combination [ж'ж'] is represented in spelling by the letter combinations зж and жж, when these combinations are part of one root, as in езжу and вожжи. When, however, the letters зж come together as a result of the compounding of a word, the combination represents a long, hard [ж], e.g. изжить (из + жить) [ижжы́т'] *to get rid of*. The pronunciation [жж] instead of [ж'ж'] is now spreading to words in which зж and жж are part of one and the same root.

EXERCISE 45.[1] Practise the following words: щи [ш'ш'и] *cabbage-soup*, счет [ш'ш'от] *bill*, плащ [плаш'ш'] *cape*, гуща [гу́ш'ш'ъ] *dregs*, пощада [паш'ш'а́дъ] *mercy*, счистить [ш'ш'йс'т'ит'] *to clean up*, резче [р'е́ш'ш'ь][2] *sharper*, вязче [в'а́ш'ш'ь][2] *stickier*, жестче[3] [жо́ш'ш'ь][2] *harder*, хлестче[3] [хл'о́ш'ш'ь][2] *more biting*; езжу [йе́ж'ж'у][2] [йэ́жжу] *I go*, вожжи [во́ж'ж'и] or [во́жжы] *reins*, жужжать [жуж'ж'а́т'][2] or [жужжа́т'] *to buzz*.

[1] The pronunciation [ш'ш'] is adopted here for щ, сч and зч though this is not to imply that this type of pronunciation is in any sense 'better' than the other variants described above.

[2] See Chapter 8 for the vowels in these words.

[3] One of the very few words containing the letter combination стч, having the same value as сч.

7

FOUR CONSONANTS

[л] AND [л']

Most English-speaking students of Russian have difficulty with hard [л] or soft [л'] or with both these consonants. Both [л] and [л'] are sounds of the *l*-type and though the RP speaker has two kinds of *l*-sound, their formation differs somewhat and their usage considerably from those of the Russian sounds. GA and Scots speakers usually have one kind of *l*-sound and may be inclined to use this *l* for both kinds of Russian *l*-sound. The two Russian sounds, therefore, must be learnt correctly as regards both formation and usage.

Sounds of the *l*-type are formed in the following manner: the tip of the tongue is placed against the teeth-ridge,[1] a space being left between the gums (or teeth) and the edge of the tongue on either side; the vocal cords vibrate, producing 'voice', and the stream of sound passes through the gaps between gums and tongue.[2]

In the foregoing description no mention has been made of the position of the main body of the tongue, except indirectly in the statement that a space is left between the gums and the sides of the tongue. As long as this space is left and the tip of the tongue is held against the teeth-ridge, the main body of the tongue can in fact adopt any vowel-position while an *l*-sound is being made.

Exercise 46. Make a prolonged *l*, combining it in turn with the resonances of the Russian vowels [и], [э], [а], [о], [у], i.e. trying to make these vowels at the same time (the lips may remain in a more or less neutral position). Do not at first make a series of separate *l*'s but make one long *l*, keeping the tongue-tip against

---

[1] Against the back of the upper teeth in some languages, though not in English and Russian.

[2] As the air-stream passes through the mouth in the formation of *l*-sounds there may or may not be friction. English and Russian *l*-sounds are not normally produced with audible friction. Sounds of the *l*-type can also be made without voice and indeed occur regularly in some languages. In English and Russian, however, such types of *l* are minor varieties, arising 'accidentally'.

the teeth-ridge and allowing the main body of the tongue to glide through the positions of the various vowels:

$$\left\{ \begin{matrix} [и] \ldots [ə] \ldots [a] \ldots [o] \ldots [y] \\ lllllllllllllllllllllllllllll \end{matrix} \right\}$$

Having practised this to your satisfaction, now make a series of separate *l*-sounds with different vowel-resonances:

$$\left\{ \begin{matrix} [ə] \\ l \end{matrix} \right\} \quad \left\{ \begin{matrix} [a] \\ l \end{matrix} \right\} \quad \left\{ \begin{matrix} [и] \\ l \end{matrix} \right\} \quad \left\{ \begin{matrix} [y] \\ l \end{matrix} \right\} \quad \left\{ \begin{matrix} [o] \\ l \end{matrix} \right\} \quad \left\{ \begin{matrix} [ы] \\ l \end{matrix} \right\}$$

The *l*-sound with the resonance of a vowel midway between that of Russian [o] and that of Russian [y] is the Russian [л]. The vowel-resonance of [л] is approximately that of the *o* in the Scots pronunciation of *home*. This type of *l*-sound is known as a 'dark' *l*.

The position of the tongue in forming [л] is: tip of tongue against teeth-ridge, middle of tongue curved downwards, so that a shallow trough is formed between the tip and back of the tongue.

The *l* heard at the end of the word *double* (in GA, Scots and RP) is very similar to Russian [л] and makes a good starting-point or even an adequate substitute for it. Scots and GA speakers use this kind of *l* in all positions whereas in RP it is used only at the end of words and before consonants.

Students who are unable to produce [л] by way of the preceding exercise should try the following method:

EXERCISE 47. Say the word *double*, prolonging the final *l*. Isolate this *l*, still prolonging it, and put a vowel after it: *llloo* (as in *moon*), *llla* (as in *father*). Do not pause between the *l* and the following vowel. If you find this difficult, begin by saying *double* with a prolonged *l* and put various vowels after it (again without pause between *l* and vowel) and then try the first part of the exercise (i.e. omitting the '*doub*' of *double*). Having practised this kind of *l*, modify it by lowering the middle of the tongue to reach the position for [л]. Now practise the following vocables: [улу], [ала], [олу], [лу], [ла], [ло].

Scots and GA speakers normally have a 'dark' *l* in all positions, as has been indicated above. The dark *l* which they use in front of vowels, however, may not be quite dark enough for Russian [л] and it is advisable for them too to practise the above exercise.

Russian [л'] is a sound not found in either RP, GA or Scots. It is formed with the tip of the tongue against the teeth-ridge and the front of the tongue pressed quite firmly up against the hard

palate. The nearest corresponding sound in RP is the *l* heard in
million, but in Russian [л'] even more of the front of the tongue is
held against the hard palate and there is, moreover, an important
distinguishing feature to Russian [л'] in the manner of releasing
the tongue. Russian [л'] has the tongue-position of [й] or the *y*
in English *yield*, while still retaining the lateral gap and the contact
of the tongue-tip against the teeth-ridge.

EXERCISE 48. Say the unbroken sequence of *l*-sounds learnt from

Exercise 47. Reverse the sequence, beginning with $\left\{ {[y] \atop l} \right\}$ and

ending with $\left\{ {[и] \atop l} \right\}$. Now complete this sequence with an *l* having

the tongue position of [й], i.e. let the front of the tongue carry on
rising through [a], [ə] and [и] and beyond. The final *l*-sound now
is [л']. Alternatively, place the tongue in position for an *l*-sound
and, while maintaining the tip of the tongue on the teeth-ridge,
deliberately push up the front of the tongue against the hard palate
into the position of [й] (or *y* in *yield*). Make an *l*-sound with the
tongue in this position. The result should be [л']. Practise: [ол'],
[ал'], [ул'], [ил'], [о́л'гъ], [у́л'дъ], [о́л'нъ], [ал'но́], [ил'ду́].

When [л'] is followed by a vowel, the front of the tongue (raised
against the hard palate in the position for [й]) is released last, so
that before the vowel is sounded a short [й]-sound is heard. A
very precise notation of the word лес *forest*, therefore, would be
[л'й͜ə͜ᵇc] but for normal purposes it is sufficient to write [л'əc].
The [л'] is completely 'soft' throughout, i.e. the front of the tongue
is against the hard palate from beginning to end.

[л'] followed by a vowel must not sound like the kind of *l* one
hears in e.g. English *leek* followed by [й] and then by the vowel.
A pronunciation which we may write as [lйəc] (for [л'əc]) sounds
particularly un-Russian. The slight [й] between [л'] and a vowel
is not heard when the vowel is [и].

EXERCISE 49. Say the [л'] learnt in the preceding exercise, prolonging it and making sure it is soft throughout. Glide from this
long [л'] into a vowel, e.g. [a], making the transition slowly at first
and allowing the intervening [й] to be clearly audible, then pronouncing the vocable more quickly, shortening the [л'] and the
[й]-glide until a syllable of 'normal' length is heard. Perform this
exercise with various vowels: [л'a], [л'o], [л'y], [л'ə].

Both [л] and [л'] occur at the end of words, before and after consonants and before and after vowels. [л], however, does not occur before [и], [э], [е] or [ь], and [л'] does not occur before [ы]. [л] also does not occur after [е], [ä], [ö] or [ÿ] (Chapter 8), since these vowels can occur only before a soft consonant. Both [л] and [л'] are represented in spelling by the letter л. When followed by и, е, ю, я or ь the letter л denotes [л'], otherwise it denotes [л]. When two letters л occur together and both are pronounced, the value of the first is the same as the value of the second.

It sometimes happens that at the end of a word [л] or [л'] is preceded by a voiceless consonant, in which case [л] or [л'] is also voiceless. Such voiceless [л] and [л'] will in most cases arise automatically in the proper place and the student need not pay particular attention to these sounds. He should, however, be careful to avoid inserting between a consonant and a final [л] or [л'] a vowel like [ъ] or [ь]—смысл [смысл] *not* [смы́съл] *sense*, мысль [мыс'л'] not [мы́с'ьл'] *thought*.

EXERCISE 50. Practise the following words: лыжи [лы́жы] *skis*, лавка [ла́фкъ] *stall*, ловко [ло́фкъ] *skilfully*, лук [лук] *onion*, волна [вална́] *wave*, холм [холм] (*not* [хо́лъм]) *hill*, палка [па́лкъ] *staff*, вол [вол] *ox*, лгун [лгун] (*not* [лъгу́н])[1] *liar*; липа [л'и́пъ] *lime-tree*, лес [л'эс] *wood*, поля [пал'а́] *fields*, лет [л'от] *flight*, люк [л'ук] *hatch*, соль [сол'] *salt*, вольно [во́л'нъ] *stand at ease!*, рояль [райа́л'] *grand-piano*, льда [л'да] (*not* [л'ъда́] or [л'ьда́])[1] *ice* (*g.sg.*); (voiceless [л] and [л']): смысл [смысл] *sense*, вопль [вопл'] *howl*, мысль [мыс'л'] *thought*.

[р] AND [р']

The Russian consonants [р] and [р'] are sounds of the *r*-type, which includes sounds of very varied modes of formation. The Russian sounds of this type are *trilled*, i.e. the tip of the tongue strikes the teeth-ridge several times in rapid succession.[2] No such trilled sound occurs in either RP or GA and, though some Scots speakers have a trilled *r*, many do not.

[1] Do not allow a vowel (akin to Russian [ь]) to come between the [л] and the [г] in [лгун] or a [ь] to come between the [л'] and the [д] in [л'да]. In these and similar words [л] and [л'] act as vowels and, phonetically, the words [лгун] and [л'да] have two syllables, the first syllable being formed simply by [л] or [л'].

[2] One cannot deliberately direct the tip of the tongue to and from the teeth-ridge with sufficient rapidity to produce [р]: the tapping of the tongue arises automatically if the tongue is held in the correct position.

The manner of formation of [p] can be described quite briefly but many English speakers find it difficult to produce the sound. To pronounce [p] the tip of the tongue is held fairly loosely against the teeth-ridge and as the air-stream passes over the tongue the tip is forced downwards slightly; it immediately returns to its initial position and is again immediately forced down, this up-and-down movement persisting as long as the tongue is held correctly and the air-stream passes over it.[1] The continual tapping of the tongue against the teeth-ridge produces the characteristic trill. The vocal cords vibrate, producing 'voice'.

The student who cannot produce a trilled [p] by simple imitation[2] or by following the description given above should try the exercise given below. Before trying the exercise, he had better forget all about his normal English *r*: attempts to adapt *r* to Russian [p] are not likely to meet with success.

Exercise 51. Say the two syllables [тъдá] with a Russian (dental) [т] and an English *d*, followed either by Russian [a] or the *a* of English *father*. Say this vocable rapidly several times in succession, making the first vowel, [ъ], as short as possible and shortening it still further as the exercise progresses. After some time, you may find that instead of a *d* you are producing a single tap of the tongue-tip against the teeth-ridge.[3] This is, in fact, one tap of a Russian [p]. If you are fortunate and reach the stage where this exercise produces two or three rapid taps of the tongue-tip, you already have a Russian [p]. If you produce only one tap at first you must concentrate on sensing how this has been done—in what way the tongue is held—and try to extend this one tap into several.

---

[1] See footnote 2, p. 49.

[2] It may be worth while pointing out that some English speakers who think they cannot imitate [p] can produce this sound if asked to 'make a noise like a motor-bike'. They then produce *brrr* or *drrr*, with a beautifully trilled *r*

[3] GA speakers often use a single such tap or flap of the tongue where *t* is written in such words as *latter* and some RP speakers do this occasionally in rapid speech. It is generally thought, mistakenly, that this tap is the 'same' as the *d* (in *ladder*, for example). That it is not is easily shown by the fact that GA speakers distinguish quite clearly *ladder* from *latter*. Many RP speakers use a similar sound between vowels and before unstressed syllables where *r* is written, as in *very*. Students who have this tapped or flapped *r*-sound may prefer to start from this sound and follow the exercise from this point.

Although Russian [p] consists of only a few taps of the tongue-tip,[1] you should not be satisfied until you can trill [p] for *several seconds*. It may take a considerable time and many repetitions of the exercise before you achieve a properly trilled [p]. Having achieved it, you should then practise it in combination with various vowels and *particularly* in front of consonants and as a final sound: [po], [pa], [ру], [ара], [оро], [орт], [арн], [урк], [ор], [ар], [ыр], etc.

[p] is represented in spelling by the letter p.

EXERCISE 52. Practise the following words: рад [рат] *glad*, ров [роф] *trench*, рог [рок] *horn*, рука [рука́] *hand*, трава [трава́] *grass*, дрова [драва́] *firewood*, друг [друк] *friend*, гора [гара́] *mountain*, дурак [дура́к] *fool*, город [го́рът] *town*, города [гърада́] *towns*, гончар [ган'ча́р] *potter*, столяр [стал'а́р] *joiner*, вор [вор] *thief*, жар [жар] *heat*, сорт [сорт] *sort*, спорт [спорт] *sport*, дерн [д'орн] *turf*, фирма [ф'и́рмъ] *firm*, ртуть [ртут'] *mercury*, ржи [ржы] *rye (g.sg.)*.

In the last two examples [p] is syllabic, i.e. these words consist phonetically of two syllables and the [p] 'acts as a vowel'. No vowel should be allowed to intervene between the [p] and the following consonant. When a preposition ending in a vowel precedes such words the [p] is no longer syllabic: изо ртути [изарту́т'и] *out of mercury*, со ржи [саржы́] *from the rye*.

At the end of a word, after a voiceless consonant, [p] is usually voiceless. The tongue is held in the normal way but the voice is silent while the air-stream issues and all that is heard is a number of voiceless taps with a fair amount of friction. Examples are: Петр [п'отр] *Peter*, смотр [смотр] *inspection*, Днепр [д'н'эпр] *Dnieper*, арбитр [арб'и́тр] *referee*.

Russian [p'] is adapted from [p] in the same way that [c'], [з'] are adapted from [c], [з], i.e. the tongue-tip is placed as for [p] but the front of the tongue is raised towards the hard palate. It will usually be found that the front of the tongue cannot be raised so high in producing [p'] as in producing [c'], [з']. If the front of the tongue is raised too high the tip of the tongue cannot vibrate so freely and the trill may be 'cut off' altogether.

Alternatively one may try to produce [p] and [й] simultaneously. The result should *not* sound merely like a succession of [p] and [й], though when a vowel follows [p'] and when [p'] is at the end of a

---

[1] Between vowels the number of taps of Russian [p] is one or at the most two. Do not prolong [p] unduly even in other positions.

word there will be a very slight trace of [й]-like sound after it, since the front of the tongue is lowered after the tip has been removed from the [p']-position. It may take just as long to develop [p'] as it took to develop [p]. [p'] should not in any case be attempted until [p] has been properly achieved. Usually, it is not possible to hold on a trilled [p'] for as long as a trilled [p] can be held but the student should nevertheless try to trill [p'] for a second or two.

[p'] is represented in spelling by the letter p (followed, of course, by и, е, я, ю or ь).

EXERCISE 53. Practise the following words: ряд [p'ат] *row*, рев [p'оф] *roar*, рюмка [p'ýмкъ] *wine-glass*, гриб [гр'ип] *mushroom*, брякать [бр'áкът] *to clatter*, пекарь [п'э́кър'] *baker*, корь [кор'] *measles*.

[p'] occurs very occasionally at the end of a word after a voiceless consonant and is then voiceless, as in вепрь [в'эпр'] *boar*.

8

SIX VOWELS AND THE DIPHTHONGS

(a) SIX VOWELS

[e]

THE Russian vowel [e] differs from the Russian vowel [ə] (Chapter 3) in being more close, i.e. the tongue is in a higher position. The vowel in English *get*, like Russian [ə], has a lower tongue position than Russian [e] and will not, therefore, serve as a substitute for Russian [e]. The French 'e-acute' (*é*) sound is very like Russian [e].

In RP such English words as *they*, *day* have a diphthong: after the initial consonant the tongue starts at a position slightly higher than the position for *e* in *get* and then glides to a position similar to that for *i* in *bit*. Students should try to isolate the starting-point of this diphthong and produce a simple, non-diphthongal vowel in this position. GA speakers often have a slightly diphthongal sound in such words as *they*, *day*. They should follow the instructions given above. Scots speakers usually have a simple vowel in *they*, *day*, formed in the position where the RP diphthong begins and they may use this vowel as a starting-point. All three types of speakers should then try to shift the simple vowel very slightly in the direction of Russian [и], i.e. try to make it slightly 'more like [и]', *without, however, letting it become diphthongal again.*

Those who find it too difficult to isolate the starting-point of the diphthong in *they*, *day* should try to make a vowel intermediate between their *e* in *get* and Russian [и], always remembering that the vowel they are aiming at—Russian [e]—is *not* a diphthong but a simple vowel. The vowel sound in RP *they*, *day* is a diphthong and will *not* serve as a substitute for Russian [e].

Whichever method is used for obtaining Russian [e], the student should practise prolonging this sound—[eeee]—without letting it become diphthongal.

Russian [e] occurs *only* before soft consonants, whereas [ə] occurs before hard consonants and as the last sound in a word.

It is important, therefore, not only that the two sounds be made correctly but also that they be used in the proper positions. If they are formed correctly but used in the wrong positions, the result sounds most un-Russian.

Russian [e] is represented in spelling by the letter e and the letter э, and there is always a soft consonant following it.

EXERCISE 54. Practise the following words: петь [п'ет'] *to sing*, сесть [с'ес'т'] *to sit down*, эти [ét'и] *these*, надеюсь [над'éйус] *I hope*, цель [цел'] *aim*, медь [м'ед'] *copper*, лечь [л'еч] *to lie down*, вещь [в'еш'ш'] *thing*.

[ä], [ö], [ÿ]

The vowels described in this section are special modifications of the vowels [a], [o], [y] respectively. They occur only between two soft consonants (including [й]). [ä] and [ö] occur only in stressed position, whereas [ÿ] may occur in stressed or unstressed position.

[ä] is more close than [a]: the tongue is slightly higher in the mouth. It is very like *a* in RP *cat*, i.e. it has a distinct [ə]-quality about it.

[ö] is made further forward in the mouth than [o], though the tongue remains at the same height and the lips preserve the same degree of rounding as for [o]. It can be reached by pronouncing [ъ] with the lips in the shape for [o].

[ö] should not be confused with the sound represented by the symbol ö in German nor with the vowels heard in French *peu* and *peur*. All these vowels are vowels of the *e*-type, with lip-rounding, and are made further forward in the mouth than is Russian [ö]. However, a student who can make one or more of these vowels and is unable to produce Russian [ö] from the directions given in the preceding paragraph may find it not so difficult to adapt either German ö or the vowel in French *peu* to Russian [ö] by raising the tongue at a point slightly further back in the mouth (by 'pulling the vowel back a little') and by having the lips *less* rounded than for the French and German sounds (i.e. in the position for Russian [o], not French or German *o*, as in Fr. *Rhône*, Gmn. *Not*).

[ÿ] is made further forward in the mouth than [y], the height of the tongue being about the same as for [y] (i.e. close for stressed [ÿ], not so close for unstressed [ÿ]).

[ÿ] may sound to English speakers rather like the word *yew* but it is wrong to substitute *'yew'* for Russian [ÿ]. The lips should be placed as for [y] while the tongue takes up the position for [ы]— an 'average' [ы], i.e. one that is not too far back and not too far forward, or an unstressed [ы], gives a reasonably good tongue position for [ÿ].

Scots speakers commonly use a vowel very like [ÿ] in such words as *pool, pull* (see Chapter 3). Such a vowel is a good substitute for [ÿ].

Russian [ÿ] should not be confused with French *u* (as in *vue*) or German *ü* (as in *Süd*). These two vowels are made further forward in the mouth than is Russian [ÿ]: they are vowels of the type of Russian [и] with lip-rounding added. They may, however, serve as starting points for [ÿ], which may be adapted from them by 'making them further back in the mouth' (though not, of course, so far back that they become simply Russian [y]).

[ä] is represented in spelling by я or by a (when this letter is preceded by ч or щ). In either case, a soft consonant follows the vowel.

[ö] is represented in spelling by e[1] (sometimes written ё). A soft consonant follows this vowel.

[ÿ] is represented in spelling by ю or by y (when this letter is preceded by ч or щ). In either case, a soft consonant follows the vowel.

EXERCISE 55. Practise the following words: ящик [йа́ш'ш'ик] *box*, пять [п'ät'] *five*, грязь [гр'äс'] *dirt*, дядя [д'а́д'ъ] *uncle*, сядь [с'ät'] *sit down!*, часть [чäс'т'] *part*, чаще [ча́ш'ш'ь] *more often*; тетя [т'о́т'ъ] *aunt*, узнаете [узнайо́т'ь] *you find out*, сосете [сас'о́т'ь] *you suck*, щечка [ш'ш'о́чкъ] *little cheek*; люди [л'у́д'и] *people*, нюнить [н'у́н'ить] *to snivel*, чучело [чу́чьлъ] *stuffed dummy*, чуять [чу́йът'] *to scent*, щурить [ш'ш'у́р'ит'] *to screw up* (the eyes), тюрьма [т'ÿр'ма́] *prison*, тюлень [т'ÿл'ен'] *seal*, сюсюкать [с'ÿс'у́кът'] *to lisp*.

All the above vowels, [e], [ä], [ö], [ÿ], as well as other vowels (except [и]) followed by a soft consonant, have in common an 'off-glide' in the nature of Russian [и]. This is to say that between any of these vowels and a following soft consonant there is a very brief suggestion of [и], a result of the fact that the tongue is approaching the position for softness of the following consonant. This glide must not be exaggerated: on no account should the

---

[1] There are a few cases where [ö] is represented by o, e.g. о почтальоне [апъчтал'о́н'ь] *about the postman*. Ср. почтальон [пъчтал'о́н] *postman*.

vowel concerned become too like one of the diphthongs described below.

THE UNSTRESSED VOWELS [и] AND [ь]

When the vowel [и] occurs in unstressed positions it sounds very much like stressed [и]. It is, however, shorter than stressed [и][1] and may be said to be somewhat 'relaxed' in comparison with stressed [и]. If the student aims at stressed [и] and concentrates on making it short in unstressed position, the 'relaxation' consequent upon the absence of stress will usually suffice to produce a close approximation to unstressed [и].

Unstressed [и] is represented in spelling by и.

The vowel [ь] is, so to speak, an unstressed version of the vowel [e][2]: it is shorter than [e] (itself intrinsically a short vowel) and is pronounced in a more relaxed fashion than [e], being slightly further back than [e]. It sounds very much like the *i* in English *bit* and students who are unable to produce a very short, lax [e] (i.e. [ь]) may use the *i* in *bit* as a perfectly adequate substitute for [ь]. A symbol distinct from [e] is used to denote [ь] in this book to prevent students from making the sound too 'full', too [e]-like. [ь] is more like [e] in the syllable immediately before the stress and when it is the last sound in a word, less clearly like [e] in all other positions.

[ь] is represented in spelling by e; by я (in positions before the stressed position); and by a (in positions before the stressed position, when a is preceded by ч or щ). (In positions *after* the stressed position я and a represent [ъ].)

In fairly fast colloquial speech the pronunciations of unstressed [и] and [ь] become more and more alike and very often, especially in positions other than the absolute final position and the one immediately in front of the stressed position, become identical, both being practically indistinguishable from the *i* in *bit*.

In view of the letters which represent unstressed [и] and [ь] these sounds will be preceded either by [й] or a soft consonant. The letters ц, ш and ж are found before e occurring in unstressed position and in this case e represents a sort of unstressed [ы], i.e. a vowel further back than [ь], and with a slightly lower tongue-

[1] It must, of course, be borne in mind that stressed [и] is itself intrinsically a short vowel, much shorter than the *ee* in English *leek* (RP and GA).

[2] *Not* [ə].

position. For this vowel it is better to use the symbol [ы] rather than [ь] so that students will not pronounce too front a vowel after [ц], [ш] and [ж].

EXERCISE 56. Practise the following words: сели [с'е́л'и] *sat down*, цели [це́л'и] *aims*, вещи [в'е́ш'ш'и] *things*, чистота [чистата́] *cleanliness*, стиляга [с'т'ил'а́гъ] '*teddy-boy*', типография [т'ипагра́ф'ийъ] *printing-house*; легли [л'ьгл'и́] *they lay down*, еще [йьш'ш'о́] *still*, щека [ш'ш'ька́] *cheek*, стена [с'т'ьна́] *wall*, два часа [два чьса́] *two o'clock*, чахотка [чьхо́ткъ] *consumption*, частота [чьстата́] *frequency*, тянуть [т'ьну́т'] *to pull*, щадить (ш'ш'ьд'и́т'] *to spare*.

The letter э in unstressed position at the beginning of a word is very often pronounced simply as unstressed [э] (an [э] slightly further back than stressed [э]), unless the stressed syllable is very far removed, when [э] will become more like [ь]. Examples are экватор [эква́тър] *equator*, экономка [эка́но́мкъ] *house-keeper*, эксперимент [э^ьксп'ьр'им'э́нт] *experiment*, элэватор [э^ьл'ьва́тър][1] *elevator*.

(b) DIPHTHONGS

All the Russian vowels described in this and preceding chapters form diphthongs, with the exception of [э]. The second part or finishing-position of Russian diphthongs is [й] and since [й] acts as a soft consonant and [э] does not occur before soft consonants there can be no sequence or diphthong [эй]. The diphthongs which occur in Russian, therefore, are: [ий], [ый], [ей], [ьй], [ай], [äй], [ой],[öй], [уй], [ÿй], [ъй].

The [й] in Russian diphthongs is much more close (i.e. the tongue is higher) than, say, the sound represented by *y* or *i* in e.g. *boy*, *toy*, *toil*: it may be thought of as a somewhat shortened version of Russian [и].[2] The vowels preceding [й] in Russian diphthongs sound just as they do before a soft consonant.

The [й] in the stressed diphthong [ий] is even closer (i.e. the tongue is higher) than in the other diphthongs: it is quite definitely a sound like *y* in *yield*. The [й] in the unstressed diphthong [ий] is usually not heard as a separate sound: its effect is heard, however, in that the unstressed [и] in this diphthong is much more

---

[1] With a clear tendency of [э] towards [ь] because of the following soft consonant.

[2] Do not, however, commit the mistake of making this into a separate syllable: [ай], [ой], etc. must not sound like [а-и], [о-и], etc.

like stressed [и] in quality, though shorter in quantity. This applies particularly to the *nom. sg. masc.* ending of soft adjectives: синий [с'и́н'и(й)] *blue*. In colloquial speech, even at normal speed, the unstressed adjectival ending written -ый is usually pronounced as a simple vowel, an unstressed [ы]: красный [кра́сны][1] *red*.

The diphthongs are represented in spelling by one or other of the letters which represent the first part of the diphthong when it occurs as a simple vowel, followed by the letter й.

Thus,   [ий] is represented by ий,

[ый]	,,	,,	,, ый (and ий after ш and ж),
[ей]	,,	,,	,, ей and эй[2].
[ьй]	,,	,,	,, ей, яй and ай (after ч and щ),
stressed [ай]	,,	,,	,, ай,
unstressed [ай]	,,	,,	,, ай and ой,
[äй]	,,	,,	,, яй and ай (after ч and щ),
[ой]	,,	,,	,, ой,
[öй]	,,	,,	,, ей
[уй]	,,	,,	,, уй,
[ÿй]	,,	,,	,, юй and уй (after ч and щ),
[ъй]	,,	,,	,, ай and ой.

EXERCISE 57. Practise the following words: кий [к'ий] *billiard-cue*, белгийский [б'ьлг'и́йск'и(й)] *Belgian*, армий [а́рм'и(й)] *armies (g.pl.)*, синий [с'и́н'и(й)] *blue*; дуй [дуй] *blow!*, уйду [уйду́] *I shall go away*, пайка [па́йкъ] *soldering*, тайна [та́йнъ] *secret*, пойду [пайду́] *I shall set off*, война [вайна́] *war*, займа [займа́] *loan (g.sg.)*, выйду [вы́йду] *I shall go out*, выйти [вы́йт'и] *to go out*, красный [кра́сны(й)] *red*, желтый [жо́лты(й)] *yellow*; большой [бал'шо́й] *big*, зной [зной] *heat*, бойня [бо́йн'ъ] *slaughter-house*, не плакай [н'ь пла́къй] *don't cry*, не разговаривай [н'ь ръзгава́р'ивъй] *don't talk*, комнатой [ко́мнътъй] *room (inst. sg.)*, с дамой [зда́мъй] *with a lady*; пейте [п'е́йт'ь] *drink!*, бейте [б'е́йт'ь] *beat!*, налейте [нал'е́йт'ь] *pour out!*, выпей [вы́п'ьй] *drink it up!*, с тетей [с'т'о́т'ьй] *with auntie*, с армией [са́рм'иьй] *with an army*, Чайковский [чьйко́фск'и(й)] *Chaikovsky*, сияй [с'ийа́й] *shine!*, чай [чай] *tea*, прощайте [праш'ш'а́йт'ь] *farewell!*, землей [з'ьмл'о́й] *land (inst.sg.)*, дюйм [д'у́йм] *inch*, дюймовка [д'у́ймо́фкъ] *inch plank*

---

[1] Of course, this does not apply to the speech of those who pronounce the ending -ый, and the -ий after к, г, х, as [ъй] (see Chapter 10).

[2] In the exclamation эй! [ей], *I say, hey there!*

9

COMBINATIONS OF CONSONANTS

(a) Voiced and Voiceless

From some of the remarks in foregoing chapters and also from some of the examples given in those chapters a certain feature of the relationship between Russian spelling and pronunciation becomes evident, namely that some letters which otherwise represent voiced consonants represent the corresponding voiceless consonants when they occur at the end of a word or before voiceless consonants. The letters concerned are, in alphabetical order, б, в, г, д, ж, з, which, in the appropriate position, represent [п], [ф], [к], [т], [ш], [с] respectively.[1] Some of these letters may also, of course, denote soft voiceless consonants in the appropriate circumstances.

Exercise 58. Read the following words, paying particular attention to the relationship between spelling and pronunciation: лоб [лоп] *forehead*, юбка [йу́пкъ] *skirt*, ров [роф] *trench*, ловкий [ло́фк'ий] *skilful*, шаг [шак] *step*, год [гот] *year*, лодка [ло́ткъ] *boat*, подпор [патпо́р] *support*, еж [йош] *hedgehog*, ножка [но́шкъ] *leg of a chair*, газ [гас] *gas*, резкость [р'э́скъс'т'] *sharpness*, подтяжки [пат'т'а́шк'и] *braces*.

The above phenomenon applies not only to single words but also to combinations of preposition plus noun, pronoun or adjective, where the appropriate sequences of consonant letters arise. Thus: без копейки [б'ъскап'е́йк'и] *without a kopeck*, из парка [испа́ркъ] *out of the park*, из того [иставо́] *from that*, из тех [ис'т'эх] *from those*, без тела [б'ьс'т'э́лъ] *without a body*.

Letters which otherwise represent voiceless consonants represent the corresponding voiced consonants if they occur before б, г, д, ж or з. Notice that the letters л, м, н, р *and* в do not affect preceding consonants in this way: voiceless consonant letters representing voiceless consonants in front of them. Some of the letters which otherwise represent voiceless consonants may represent *soft* voiced consonants if the following voiced consonant is soft.

[1] For the value of г before к and ч in certain words see Chapter 10.

This phenomenon, like the preceding one, also affects combinations of preposition plus noun or adjective,[1] where the appropriate sequences of consonant letters arise.

EXERCISE 59. Read the following words, paying particular attention to the relationship between spelling and pronunciation: к дому [гдо́му] *to the house*, к женщине [гже́н'ш'ш'ин'ь] *to the woman*, сдача [зда́чъ] *change*, сделать [з'д'э́лът'] *to do*, отбор [адбо́р] *selection*, отделать [ад'д'э́лът'] *to finish off*, молотьба [мълад'ба́] *threshing*, пастьба [паз'д'ба́][2] *pasturage*, от заместителя [ад зъм'ьс'т'ӣт'ьл'ъ] *from the deputy*, от девушка [ад'д'э́вушкъ] *from the girl*, с замка [ззáмкъ] *from the castle*. But свой [свой] *one's own*, с вами [свáм'и] *with you*, слой [слой] *layer*, трава [травá] *grass*, от руки [атрук'й́] *from the hand*, смычок [смычо́к] *violin-bow*, с мокроты [смъкраты́] *from dampness*, пятно [п'ьтно́] *stain*, от нас [атнáс] *from us*.

(*b*) PLOSIVES PLUS OTHER CONSONANTS

The sounds [п], [б], [т], [д], [к], [г] and their soft counterparts are formed by placing the lips or tongue in the appropriate position, holding that position for a brief space of time and then suddenly releasing it. They are known as 'plosives' and the releasing of the lips or tongue is the 'plosion' of these consonants.

When plosives are followed by other consonants there are certain points to be observed wherein Russian pronunciation and English pronunciation are either similar or dissimilar. Thus, in both English and Russian, when two identical plosives occur together, there is no release or plosion of the first one. The closed position—or 'stop'—of the plosive is held for double the normal space of time before the release or plosion occurs. Thus there is only one plosion of the [т]'s in оттуда [атту́дъ] *from there* and of the *t*'s in *set-to*, just as there is only one plosion of the [д]'s in поддавать [пъддавáт'] *to add to* and of the *d*'s in *good-day*. This applies equally to sequences of [пп], [бб], [кк], [гг] and sequences of identical soft plosives.

Moreover, when *t* is followed by *ch* in English, as in *dirt-cheap*, there is no individual release of the *t*: it merges into the following

---

[1] It cannot affect combinations of preposition plus pronoun since there are no pronouns in Russian beginning with б, г, д, ж or з.

[2] Notice that both the с and the т represent voiced consonants in front of б: voicing passes back to all the consonants before б, г, д, ж or з.

ch and there is only one release, that of the *ch*. The same holds good in Russian when т or д is followed by ц or ч. Before ц both т and д will represent [т], a [т], moreover, which is no longer dental but made on the teeth-ridge, like [ц] itself, and there is no separate release of this [т]. [тц] in отцы [атцы́] *fathers*, therefore, is like a 'long' [ц], i.e. a [ц] in which the first element, the stop, is held on for twice the normal length of time. Before ч both т and д will represent a special kind of soft [т'], identical with the first element of [ч], without its own individual release. [т'ч] in отчий [о́т'чий] *father's*, therefore, is like a 'long' [ч], i.e. a [ч] in which the first element is held on for twice the normal length of time.

In the most usual pronunciation of English there is in general no separate release of plosives which are followed by other dissimilar plosives or by *ch* or *j*. Thus, in pronouncing *act* the back of the tongue does not leave the roof of the mouth (where it is placed for the pronunciation of the *k*-sound, represented by *c*) until the *t* has been pronounced. Similarly, the *k*-sound, represented by *ck*, in *back-chat* is not released before the *ch* is pronounced. Again, the *d* in *feed-back* is often not released before the *b* is pronounced.

The case is different in Russian. When two unlike plosives occur together, the first *must* be fully released before the second is pronounced. There are thus two separate plosions. The result of this in the case of voiced plosives is that there occurs between dissimilar hard plosives a very short sound of the nature of [ъ], and between dissimilar soft voiced plosives a very short sound in the nature of [ь]. In neither case is this 'accidental' sound to be exaggerated so that it forms a separate syllable.

The same holds good in Russian when plosives other than [т] and [т'] precede [ц] and [ч]: the plosive must be fully released before [ц] or [ч] is pronounced.

In the following examples a plus sign (+) is inserted after the first plosive in the phonetic transcriptions to draw attention to the fact that these plosives must be fully released before the next sound is pronounced: акт [ак + т] *act*, когда [каг + да́] *when*, отбор [ад + бо́р] *selection*, где [г + д'э] *where*, обтирать [ап + т'ира́т'] *to wipe*, юбка [йу́п + къ] *skirt*, обдумать [аб + ду́мът'] *to think over*, подпора [пат + по́ръ] *support*, купцу [куп + цу́] *merchant* (*dat.sg.*), тягчайший [т'ьк + ча́йшы] *most weighty*.

When *d* or *t* occurs before *l* or *n* in the most usual pronunciation of English, the *d* or *t* is not released in the normal way: the stop is made in the ordinary way but the release does not occur until the *l* or *n* is finished. Examples of this occur in the following words: *riddle, little, padlock, catnip, mutton, garden*.[1] A similar procedure takes place when *p* or *b* is followed by *m*: *topmost* (not *top + most*), *cabman* (not *cab + man*).

The same practice is correct in Russian too: продлить [прад'л'йт'] (not [прад' + л'йт']) *to prolong*, поднос [паднóс] (not [пад + нóс]) *tray*, обморок [óбмърък] (not [óб + мърък]) *swoon*. In English, a similar phenomenon occurs with the groups *kn*, *gn*, *tm*, *dm*, *pn*, *bn*, e.g. *Cockney* (not *Cock + ney*), *agnostic* (not (*ag + nostic*), *utmost* (not *ut + most*), *madman* (not *mad + man*), *Stepney* not *Step + ney*), *hobnail* (not *hob + nail*). With regard to the corresponding groups in Russian, such a practice is *incorrect*: the plosives in these groups must be fully released before the sound represented by following м or н is pronounced. Again, the result will be, where voiced consonants are concerned, a very short intervening [ъ]-sound in the case of hard consonants and a very short intervening [ь]-sound in the case of soft consonants. Neither of these two 'accidental' sounds must be exaggerated so that it forms an extra syllable. The following words exemplify some of the combinations: окно [ак + нó] *window*, гибнуть [г'йб + нут'] *to perish*, тьма [т' + ма] *darkness*, подмога [пад + мóгъ] *help*, отмывать [ат + мывáт'] *to wash off*, ведьма [в'éд' + мъ] *witch*, книга [к + н'йгъ] *book*, гнуть [г + нут'] *to bend*, гнилой [г + н'илóй] *rotten*, топнуть [тóп + нут'] *to stamp*, догма [дóг + мъ] *dogma*, лакмус [лáк + мус] *litmus*.

(*c*) SOFTNESS OF CONSONANTS OCCURRING TOGETHER

It will have been seen from some of the examples given in preceding chapters that, often enough, when there are two consonants together and the spelling indicates that the second consonant is soft, the first consonant is soft, too. This phenomenon may be called 'regressive softening', a term which indicates that the softness of one consonant passes back or regresses, so to speak, to a preceding consonant. All native Russian speakers use regressive

[1] It must be admitted that there is a tendency among some speakers of English to release the *t* and *d* in *mutton* and *garden* and pronounce a short, 'obscure' vowel before the following *n*. This is common among many Scots. However, all such speakers pronounce a word like *catnip* without a separate plosion for the *t*.

softening to some extent but there are many details in which the practice varies from speaker to speaker.

There are, however, some instances of regressive softening which are shared by all native Russian speakers. These instances may be thought of as the basic, minimal requirements for a good pronunciation of Russian. Most of them are, moreover, instances of regressive softening which, as it were, are soon likely to arise spontaneously even in the pronunciation of a non-native speaker.

When т, д, н, с or з combines with т, д, н, с or з and the second letter denotes a soft consonant, then so does the first. There are possible then twenty-five such combinations, some of which are illustrated in the exercise below. It must be borne in mind, of course, that the voicing and unvoicing phenomena which were described in the last chapter operate here too. It has already been pointed out elsewhere that when two identical consonants occur together in Russian they become in fact one long consonant. Thus, in [т'т'], [д'д'], and also in [тт], [дд], the tip of the tongue is released once only—at the end of the 'pair' of consonants.

Examples: сесть [с'éс'т'] *to sit down*, оттепель [óт'т'ьп'ьл'] *thaw*, здесь [з'д'ес'] *here*, сделать [з'д'э́лът'] *to do*, отсюда [ат'с'у́дъ] *hence, from here*, подседельник [път'с'ьд'éл'н'ик] *saddle-girth*, мясник [м'áс'н'ик] *butcher*, вонзить [ван'з'и́т'] *to plunge in*, снег [с'н'эк] *snow*.

The letters т, д, н, с, з also represent soft consonants before л when the latter represents a soft consonant: след [с'л'эт] *trace*, продлить [прад'л'и́т'] *to prolong*, обозлить [абаз'л'и́т'] *to annoy*, сонливый [сан'л'и́вы] *sleepy*, петля [п'éт'л'ъ] *loop*.

с and з may represent soft consonants before р, when р denotes a soft consonant: среда [с'р'ьдá] *Wednesday*, зрелый [з'р'э́лы] *ripe*.

т, д, н represent soft consonants before ч and щ, which always represent soft consonants.[1] In these cases т and д will represent a soft consonant like the [т']-element at the beginning of [ч], so that [т'ч] will sound like a 'long' [ч] and [т'ш'ш'] or [т'ш'ч] will sound like [чш'ш'] or [чш'ч]. Examples: отчасти [óт'чьс'т'и] *partially*, тщательно [т'ш'ш'áт'ьл'нъ] *thoroughly*, подчинить [пот'чин'и́т'] *to subject*, кончить [кóн'чит'] *to finish*, гонщик [гóн'ш'ш'ик] *racer*.

The letters which represent consonants formed with the lips or with the teeth and lower lip may represent soft consonants of this type if they are followed by another letter representing a soft consonant

[1] Except for ч in a few words (see Chapter 10).

of this type, i.e. both letters may represent soft consonants in the combinations of п, б, м, ф or в with п, б, м, ф or в followed by и, е, я, ю or ь. Examples: обвинитель [аб'в'ин'и́т'ьл'] *prosecutor*, ввести [в'в'ьс'т'и́] *to introduce*, вместе [в'м'ес́'т'ь] *together*, вперед [ф'п'ьр'о́т] *forward*, имбирь [им'б'и́р'] *ginger*, о рифме [ар'и́ф'м'ь] *concerning rhyme*.

The letters с and з, when they occur before ч or щ, represent [ш']. Before щ this sound will, so to speak, be absorbed into the [ш'ш'] or [ш'ч] represented by щ. Examples: счастье [ш'ш'а́с'т'йь] *happiness*, счищать [ш'ш'иш'ш'а́т'] *to clean up*, расщепить [ръш'ш'ьп'и́т'] *to split*, приказчик [пр'ика́ш'ш'ик] *shop-assistant*.

When т, д, с or з occurs before a letter representing a soft consonant formed with the lips or the lower lip and teeth, the tendency nowadays is to make the appropriate dental or teeth-ridge consonant hard. There are, however, a number of words in which these consonants are commonly made soft. Some of these are: две [д'в'э] *two*, медведь [м'ьд'в'ет́'] *bear*, дверь [д'в'ер́'] *door*, четверть [чет́'в'ьрт'] *quarter*, четверо [чет́'в'ьрꙏ] *four*, зверь [з'в'ер'] *wild animal*, лезвие [л'ез́'в'ийь] *blade*, Дмитрий [д'м'и́тр'ий] *Dimitry*, свет [с'в'эт] *light*.

READING RULES I

(a) The Phonetic Value of some Single Letters and Groups of Letters

Some of the reading rules given in this chapter repeat, in a different form, information which has been given in preceding chapters. Others treat of points which have either only been touched upon or not treated at all in preceding chapters.

(i) Some Vowel Letters

о in unstressed positions has the value of the letter а (i.e. [a] immediately before the stress, otherwise [ъ]) but in a few cases о in unstressed position has the value [о]. (See next chapter.)

я in stressed positions has the value [a] or [ä] preceded by [й] or a soft consonant. In positions *before* the stress it has the value [ь], whereas in positions *after* the stress it has the value [ъ]. In both cases a soft consonant or [й] will precede it: пяти [п'ьт'и́] *five* (*gen.sg.*), but поля [по́л'ъ] *field* (*gen.sg.*).

и has the value [и] in initial position, except in the words их, им, ими (*gen., acc., prep.; dat.; inst. of* они), where it may have the value [йи]: [йих], [йим], [йи́м'и].

When the preceding word ends in a hard consonant and there is no pause between the two words, then initial и of the second word has the value [ы]: сын и дочь [сын ы доч] *son and daughter,* он видел Ивана [он в'и́д'ъл ыва́нъ] *he saw John.* This phenomenon should be particularly noted where the first word is a preposition: от ига [аты́гъ] *from the yoke,* с ивы [сы́вы][1] *from the willow.* When и is preceded by ц, ш or ж it always has the value [ы]: цинк [цынк] *zinc,* шить [шыт'] *to sew,* жить [жыт'] *to live.* This point should be carefully observed, as it is one which beginners frequently forget.

е in stressed positions has the value of [е] before a soft consonant, otherwise [э]. In some words it has the value [о] or [ö]

---

[1] Compare the perfectives of such verbs as играть [игра́т'] *to play* and искать [иска́т'] *to seek*: сыграть [сыгра́т'], сыскать [сыска́т'].

65

(preceded by soft consonant, [ш], [ж] or [й]): елка [йо́лкъ] *fir-tree*, тетя [т'о́т'ъ] *aunt*, лед [л'от] *ice*, шелк [шолк] *silk*, желтый [жо́лты] *yellow*. In unstressed positions e usually has the value [ь]. Some speakers, however, pronounce the final e of the *nom. sg. neuter* of adjectives and nouns as if it were я, and in many foreign loan-words of recent origin e in unstressed positions often has a value more like [e] than [ь].

As a general rule the consonants which can precede [e] are [й], or a soft consonant, or one of the hard sounds [ц], [ш], [ж]. In many recent loan-words, however, hard [т], [д], [с], [з], [р] (and, very occasionally, hard lip-consonants) are found before e. These cases are treated below, in the next chapter.

(ii) Some Consonant Letters

н has the value of [н] or [н']. When it occurs before [к], [г] or [х], it does *not* have the value that *n* has in such English words as *bank*, *sang*, i.e. an *n* formed in the same place as *k* or *g*. н always signifies a *tongue-tip* consonant in Russian: цинк [цынк] *zinc* (*not* like the *n* in English *zinc*), английский [англ'и́йск'ий] *English* (*not* like the *n*'s in English *angling*).

ц always represents a *hard* consonant, no matter what vowel letter follows. There is no such thing as a soft [ц] in Russian. Students should observe this carefully, since there is a tendency among beginners to make a soft [ц] when the letter e or и follows the letter ц, as often occurs.

ш and ж, too, always represent hard sounds (except optionally in the cases noted below) no matter whether и, e, or ь follows.[1] The ь in ложь, вошь, etc. and the second person singular of the present tense (читаешь, etc.) has no phonetic significance whatsoever.

(iii) Some Combinations of Letters

ое, ее, ые, ие. In the pronunciation of some speakers the letter e in these adjective endings has the value [ъ] . It is usually older speakers who have this feature of pronunciation and even among these speakers the endings ые and ие are more likely to be pronounced [ыйь] and [ийь] respectively. The pronunciation of e as [йь] in all these endings is now regarded as 'correct': красное

---

[1] ю is occasionally found after ш and ж (e.g. парашютист, жюри) but the consonants remain hard.

[кра́снъйъ] and [кра́снъйь] *red*, синее [с'и́н'ъйъ] and [с'и́н'ьйь] *blue*, красные [кра́сныйь], синие [с'и́н'ийь], etc.

It should be noted that, since the final two vowels in each of the words синее and синие are in very weakly stressed positions and are, moreover, already very similar, they will tend in fairly rapid speech to become identical, both words being pronounced approximately [с'и́н'ьь], with elision of [й]. Indeed, in rapid speech the two vowels may coalesce into [и], thus: [с'и́н'и]. (See also next section.) ие as a *noun* ending has the value [ийь] in careful speech: знание [зна́н'ийь] *knowledge*. In speech at normal speed, however, the [и] is usually lost: [знан'йь].[1] Indeed throughout the various declensional forms of such words as знание, the и often has no more significance than a soft sign, thus: знания [зна́н'йъ] (*gen.sg.*), знанием [зна́н'йьм] (*inst.sg.*). In the *loc.sg.* a careful pronunciation would be знании [зна́н'ийи] but at normal speed this form would sound more like [зна́н'йи].[2]

ия. In the forms of feminine nouns in -ия the [и] is also subject to the 'reduction' described in the preceding section, though not quite as extensively. Thus, in the forms where и is followed by я, e.g. *nom.sg.* армия *army*, *dat.pl.* армиям, *inst.pl.* армиями, *loc.pl.* армиях, the [и] does not usually disappear entirely, whereas in forms where и is followed by и or й the ending sounds simply like [и] in fairly rapid speech: армии [а́рм'и][2] (*gen.*, *dat.*, *loc. sg.*, *nom.pl.*), армий [а́рм'и][2](*gen.pl.*). In the *inst.sg.* too the [и] is quite likely to be reduced: армией [а́рм'йьй] (instead of the careful [а́рм'ийьй]).

Two vowel letters occurring together: apart from the cases described above, the occurrence of two vowel letters together is quite common in Russian. The second vowel letter is almost always a 'soft' vowel symbol (и, е, ю or я) and has the value [й] plus the appropriate vowel sound. Such combinations are very common in the forms of first conjugation verbs, e.g. читать *to read*: читаю, читаешь, читает, etc. Careful pronunciation of such forms would be: [чита́йу], [чита́йьш], [чита́йьт], etc. At normal speed, however, forms with е in the spelling are more likely to be pronounced with [и] than with [йь], thus: [чита́иш], [чита́ит], etc. In general,

---

[1] Some speakers pronounce the final е in such words as знание with the value [ъ].

[2] In these forms the [и] is usually somewhat longer and more clearly [и]-like in quality than an ordinary unstressed [и].

it is to be noted that [й] occurring between two vowels in Russian, when at least the second vowel is unstressed, is very weakly articulated and may disappear altogether. When it does disappear, however, it will usually leave a trace on the following vowel (in effect it 'coalesces' with the following vowel) by moving it more towards the position for [и]. This effect has been shown in e.g. [читáит], where the [й], though it has disappeared, has 'moved' the [ь] (ср. [читáйьт]) to the position of [и]. Similarly, читаю may sound like [читáÿ], where [ÿ] is nearer to [и] than is [у].

Sometimes, in recent loan-words, where the letter e follows another vowel-letter and is in stressed position, it represents simply [э] or [е] without a preceding [й]. An example of this is диета [д'иэ́тъ] *diet*. A similar phenomenon may also occur when the second of two vowel letters in a loan-word is и, e.g. деизм [д'ьи́зм] or [д'еи́зм] *deism*.

ь after a consonant letter indicates that the consonant is to be pronounced soft. It does not, however, affect ш and ж, which always represent hard consonants. (It does not occur at all after ц.) When it occurs between a consonant letter and a 'soft' vowel letter its significance is that the consonant (other than [ш] or [ж]) is soft and that [й] precedes the following vowel: костью [кóс'т'йу] *bone* (*inst.sg.*), льет [л'йот] *pours*. In e.g. ложью *lie* (*inst.sg.*), вошью *louse* (*inst.sg.*) the soft sign indicates that the following vowel is preceded by [й]: [лóжйу], [вóшйу].

The effect of the soft sign occurring between п, б, в or м and a soft vowel letter is: [п'], [б'], [в'] or [м'] plus 'fricative [й]' plus the appropriate vowel-sound. A 'fricative [й]' is a [й] in which the tongue is raised so close to the hard palate that during the first part of [й] friction is clearly audible.

ъ is of much rarer occurrence than ь. In the modern orthography it never occurs at the end of a word (as it very frequently did in the old orthography) but only between a consonant letter and a 'soft' vowel letter. Here, its function is to indicate the presence of [й] before the following vowel sound. If the preceding letter is с or з the appropriate consonant may be pronounced soft, whereas other letters before ъ represent hard consonants. (There is a tendency among younger speakers to pronounce hard [с] and [з] before ъ.) Examples: съесть [с'йес'т']¹ *to eat up*, съемка [с'йóмкъ] *survey*, изъятие [из'йáт'йь] *exclusion*, разъединение

¹ Compare сесть [с'ес'т'] *to sit down*.

[ръз'йьд'ин'éн'йь] *dissociation*, отъезд [атйэ́ст] *departure*, подъем [падйо́м] *rise*, объявление [абйьвл'éн'йь] *declaration*.

гк, гч. In words derived from the bases легк- *light, easy*, and мягк- *soft*, г has the value [х] before [к] and may have the value [х'] before [к'] and [ч]: легко [л'ьхко́] *easily*, мягко [м'а́хкъ] *quietly*, легкий [л'о́х'к'ий] *easy*, мягкий [м'а́х'к'ий] *soft*, облегчение [абл'ьх'чéн'йь] *facilitation*, смягчение [с'м'ьх'чéн'йь] *softening*. But cp. тягчайший [т'ькча́йшы] *most weighty*.

чт has the value [шт], not [чт], in the word что *what* and most of its derivatives: что [што] *what*, что-то [што́-тъ] *something*, что-нибудь [што́-н'ибут'] *anything*, кое-что [ко̀йь-што́][1] *something, a little*. The word нечто *something* is usually pronounced with the normal value of ч: [н'о́чтъ] but что preceded by не and a preposition (when it has the meaning *nothing*) is pronounced [штъ]: не за что [н'э́ зъ штъ] *for nothing*. Similarly, что is pronounced [што́] in the phrase ни за что [н'и за што́] *not for anything*, whereas [н'ичто́] and [н'ишто́] are both heard for ничто *nothing*. Note that что as a conjunction (*that*) is pronounced [штъ] and that the conjunction чтобы *in order that* is pronounced [што́бы] or, more commonly, [штъбы].

чн. In this combination ч usually has its normal value [ч] but there are one or two words where it commonly has the value [ш]. Among these words are скучно [ску́шнъ] *boring*, конечно [кан'э́шнъ] *of course*, пустячный [пус'т'а́шны] *trivial*, прачечная [пра́чьшнъйъ] *laundry*, яичница [йьйшн'ицъ] *egg-dish, omelette, etc.* It should be added, however, that there is now a tendency among younger speakers to pronounce these words with [ч]. Patronymics in -ична are usually pronounced with [ш]: Саввична [са́в'ишна], Никитична [н'ик'и́т'ишнъ].

щн. The letter щ usually has the value [ш'ш'] or [ш'ч] (Chapter 6) but when it is followed by н (representing [н] or [н']) it usually represents a *short soft* [ш']: мощный [мо́ш'ны] *powerful*, изящный [из'а́ш'ны] *elegant*, сокровищница [сакро́в'иш'н'ицъ] *treasure-house*. This shortening of [ш'ш'] into [ш'] sometimes occurs *after* consonants: вообще [ваапш'э́] *in general*, община [о́пш'инъ] *community*. In fairly rapid speech [ш'ш'] is shortened at the end of a word after a weakly stressed syllable: товарищ [тава́р'иш'] *comrade*, whereas in e.g. вещь *thing* it is less likely to be shortened: [в'еш'ш']

[1] With the principal stress on [што́] and a secondary stress on [ко̀йь].

сч, зч, сщ, зщ. All four of these combinations represent [ш'ш'] (or [ш'ч]), whether they occur within a word or arise at the juncture of a preposition and a following word. Examples: счастливый [ш'ш'ьс'л'и́вы] *happy*, с чем [ш'ш'эм] [ш'чэм] *with what*, с человеком [ш'чьлав'о́към] *with a person*, резче [р'е́ш'ш'ь] [р'е́ш'чь] *sharper*, из чашки [иш'ча́шк'и] *out of the cup*, расщелина [ръш'ш'ьл'и́нъ] *chink, crevice*, из щели [иш'ш'е́л'и] *out of the crack*. To pronounce с and з in these combinations as [с'] or [з'] is pedantic or over-precise.

сш, зш, сж, зж, жж. Of these combinations, the first two are pronounced [шш], the last three [жж], i.e. long [ш] and long [ж] respectively. In all except a few cases these combinations arise as a result of a prefix or a suffix being added to a root or at the juncture of preposition and following word. The few exceptional cases concern зж and жж, which also occur within roots. They may then be pronounced [ж'ж'], though even in these cases [жж] is now accepted as correct. (For examples see Chapter 6.) To pronounce с and з as [с] or [з] in these combinations is pedantic or over-precise.

жд. ж and ш, it has been stated, represent hard consonants except in the few optional cases described in Chapter 6. Words ending in -ждь, however, call for special comment. The word дождь *rain*, for example, is often pronounced as if it were spelt дощ, i.e. [дош'ш'], while the cases other than the *nom-acc.* are pronounced with a long, soft [ж'ж']: дождя [даж'ж'а́] (*gen.sg.*). Such pronunciations were formerly considered the only correct forms. Nowadays, however, it is considered equally correct to pronounce this word as the spelling indicates, i.e. [дошт'], [дажд'а́], etc., though [дош'ш'] is heard more frequently than [дошт'].

(b) Double Consonants

Double consonants are of common occurrence in Russian. Although they are called 'double' consonants, they are in fact *lengthened* consonants. Thus a double plosive consists of a stop element which is twice the length of the normal stop, followed by a single release. A double [с] or [з] or [ш], etc., consists simply of [с] or [з] or [ш], etc., held on for twice the normal length of time.

As a general rule, double consonants are pronounced so, if the letters indicating them belong to different parts of the word, e.g. prefix and root, root and suffix: оттащит [атташ'ш'и́т] *he will drag away,* отдавать [аддава́т'] *to reflect,* ввоз [ввос] *import,* туманный [тума́нны] *misty.* This applies equally if the first consonant letter belongs to a preposition: от тех [ат'т'э́х] *from those,* в воде [ввад'э́] *in the water,* в форме [ффо́рм'ь] *in the shape.*

When double consonant letters occur within a root, then usually a double consonant is pronounced: группа [гру́ппъ] *group,* масса [ма́ссъ] *mass,* ванна [ва́ннъ] *bath.* There are, however, some exceptions to this. Among the commoner of these are: ассоциация [асъцыа́цыйъ] *association,* территория [т'ьр'ито́р'ийъ] *territory,* аннулировать [анул'и́ръвът'] *to annul,* баллон [бало́н] *balloon,* баллотировать [бълат'и́ръвът'] *to vote,* беллетристика [б'ьл'ь-тр'йс'т'икъ] *belles-lettres,* грамматика [грама́т'икъ] *grammar,* аккуратный [акура́тны] *precise, punctual.*

When double consonant letters occur at the end of a root and are followed by a suffix beginning with a consonant, then usually only one of the double consonant letters is pronounced: группка [гру́пкъ] *small group,* классный [кла́сны] *class.* Double consonant letters at the end of a word are usually pronounced as a single consonant: ватт [ват] *watt,* металл [м'ьта́л] *metal.*

The adjectival suffix -ский often occurs after roots ending in с or з. In such cases a double consonant is pronounced in less common words, whereas in more common words only a single [с] is sounded: русский [ру́ск'и] *Russian,* французский [францу́ск'и] *French.*

A single [с] is pronounced where сс is written in the words искусство [иску́ствъ] *art* and искуственный [иску́ств'ьны] *artificial.* The second example also illustrates the fact that even at rapid conversation speed the double нн in the ending -енный may be and usually is pronounced as a single [н], if the e is not in stressed position. Other examples are: художественный [худо́-жыств'ьны] *artistic,* общественный [апш'ш'э́ств'ьны] *social.* Compare, with e in stressed position, благословенный [блъгъ-слав'э́нны] *blesséd,* вдохновенный [вдъхнав'э́нны] *inspired,* уговоренный [угъвар'о́нны] *persuaded,* принесенный [пр'и-н'ьс'о́нны] *brought.*

Similarly, when the a in the ending -анный is not stressed, the нн may represent a single [н] in fairly rapid speech: написанный [нап'и́съны] *written,* прочитанный [прачи́тъны] *read,* but данный [да́нны] *given,* нежданный [н'ьжда́нны] *unexpected.*

In cases where double consonant letters arise as a result of the

F

combination of preposition and following noun, pronoun or adjective a double consonant is pronounced if the initial consonant of the noun, pronoun or adjective is followed immediately by a vowel: с сестрой [с'с'ьстро́й] *with sister,* к кому [ккаму́] *to whom,* с задатком [ззада́ткъм] *with a deposit,* от тяжелого [ат'-т'ьжо́лъвъ] *from the heavy* . . . .[1] When, however, the second word begins with two consonants, the double consonant letter arising as a result of the combination with a preposition may represent merely a single consonant: с слугой [слуго́й], or, in careful speech, [сслуго́й] *with a servant,* к красивой [крас'и́въй], or, possibly, in precise speech, [ккрас'и́въй] *to the beautiful* . . . , в врага [врага́], or [ввpaга́] *against the enemy.*

Triple consonants do not occur in Russian: triple consonant letters arising as a result of the combination of a preposition and a word beginning with a double consonant are pronounced as double consonants. Thus с ссудой [ссу́дъй] *with a loan,* из ссоры [иссо́ры] *from the quarrel,* в ввозе [вво́з'ь] *in the import.*

(c) Multiple Consonant Groups

Many Russian words have three or more consonant letters together in the middle or at the end.[2] In some such combinations of multiple consonant letters all the consonants are pronounced, in others one of the consonants may be omitted, while in others one of the consonants must be omitted.

стк, здк. In these combinations all the letters are pronounced: [стк], the [т] being fully articulated before the [к], i.e. [ст + к]. Examples: жесткий [жо́стк'и] *hard,* поездка [пайэ́сткъ] *trip,* невестка [н'ьв'э́сткъ] *bride.*

вск. All the letters are pronounced in this combination: отцовский [атцо́фск'ий] *father's,* Московский [маско́фск'ий] *Muscovite.*

шск, жск. All the letters are pronounced in these combinations: чешский [чэ́шск'ий] *Czech,* латышский [латы́шск'ий] *Latvian,* волжский [во́лшский] *of the Volga,* Рижский [р'и́шск'ий] *of Riga.*

стся, сться, зться. All the consonants are pronounced in these combinations. (See next chapter.)

---

[1] N.B.: *not* [съ с'ьстрой], [къ каму́], etc.

[2] One or two such words have been discussed in the preceding section on double consonants.

нтк, ндк. All the consonants are pronounced in these combinations; студентка [студ'э́нткъ] *woman student*, аспирантка [асп'ира́нткъ] *woman post-graduate student*. In one or two words of pre-Revolutionary origin the [т] may be omitted: голландка [гала́нкъ] *Dutch stove*, гувернантка [гув'ьрна́нкъ] *governess*, but the modern tendency is to pronounce the [т] even in these words.

здн. In many common words with this combination the д is not pronounced: поздно [по́зно] *late*, праздник [пра́з'н'ик] *holiday*, звездный [зв'о́зны] *starry*. In more 'learned' words with this combination the [д] may be sounded, especially when the pronunciation is fairly careful. In this case, since [д] is not released before [н] (see above, Chapter 9), all that will be heard will be the closure or stop of [д] between [э] and [н]. Examples: бездна [б'э́зднъ] *abyss*, безвозмездный [б'ьзвазм'э́здны] *gratuitous*.

стл. As a general rule it may be stated that when и follows this combination then the т is not pronounced, otherwise it is pronounced. Thus: счастливый [ш'ш'ьс'л'и́вы] *happy*, совестливый [со́в'ьс'л'ивы] *conscientious*, but костлявый [кас'т'л'а́вы] *bony*, постлать [пастла́т'] *to spread*. Wherever the т is sounded, it will of course be without an independent release: only the closure will be heard between the sounds represented by с and л.

нтск, ндск. In general, all the consonants in these combinations are pronounced: гигантский [г'ига́нтск'ий] *gigantic*, финляндский [ф'ин'л'а́нтский] *Finnish*. In such words as these the combinations тс and дс may be pronounced [ц]. The words голландский *Dutch* and Аландский (as in Аландские острова —*the Aland Islands*) are commonly heard without [т]: [гала́нск'ий], [ала́нск'ий].

вств, фств. All four consonants in the combination вств are always pronounced (e.g. нравственный [нра́фств'ьны] *moral*, except in words derived from чувств- and здравств- where the first в is not sounded: чувство [чу́ствъ] *feeling*, чувствовать [чу́ствъвът'] *to feel*, чувствительный [чуств'и́т'ьл'ны] *sensitive*, здраствуйте [здра́ствуйт'ь][1] *How-d'ye-do*. The combination фств is rare: шефствовать [шэ́фствъвът'] *to patronise*. The first в is not pronounced in the rare combination лвств: безмолвствовать [б'ьзмо́лствъвът'] *to remain silent*.

стн. т is not pronounced in this combination: местный [м'э́сны] *local*, устный [у́сны] *oral*, свистнуть [с'в'и́снут'] *to*

[1] Pronounced rapidly, this word sounds like [здра́с'т'ь].

whistle, шестнадцать [шыснáцът'], [шыснáтцът']¹ *sixteen*, кре-
постник [кр'ьпас'н'ѝк] *serf-owner*.

стск. т is not pronounced in this combination: марксистский
[маркс'ѝсск'ий] *marxist*, лейбористский [льйбар'ѝсск'ий]
socialist.²

рдц. д is not pronounced in this combination: сердце [с'э́рцы]³
heart, сердцевина [с'ьрцывѝнъ]³ *core, pith*.

лнц. In this combination the л is not pronounced: солнце
[со́нцы]³ *sun*. Note that in солнечный *solar* the л *is* pronounced:
[со́лн'ьчны].

сткл. The word склянка *phial, bell* (in the nautical time system) is sometimes found in the spelling стклянка. In this case
the т is not pronounced: [скл'анкъ].

---

¹ [тц] is heard in a careful pronunciation of this word.
² Referring to the British Labour Party.
³ Some pronounce [ъ], instead of [ы], in these words.

READING RULES II

(a) SECONDARY STRESS AND UNSTRESSED WORDS

As a general rule, each word in Russian has a single stressed syllable. Very often, the nature not only of the vowel in the stressed syllable but also of the vowels in other syllables depends on the location of the stress: город [го́ръът] *town*, ср. города [гърада́] *towns*, городовой [гъръдаво́й] *policeman*.[1] It frequently happens that in sentences words lose their normal stress, i.e. the stress they have when spoken in isolation. When this happens, however, the quality of the vowels in the word remains more or less the same as if the word were spoken in isolation. Thus the word была *was* (*fem.*), when pronounced on its own, has stress on the second syllable—[была́]—but in the sentence Девушка была в городе *the girl was in the town* there is no stress on the word была. Nevertheless, it is pronounced with a final [a]: [д'э́вушкъ была в го́ръд'ь]. In this book, however, stress is marked on all words of more than one syllable which, when spoken on their own, have a stressed syllable. There are just one or two polysyllabic words which may, in fairly fast speech, have no stress and in which the vowels do not remain the same as when the words are spoken on their own. An example of this is the word говорит *says*, which would normally be pronounced [гъвар'и́т] but, when interposed in a sentence, may be pronounced as: [гъвъ́р'ит], as in Девушка, говорит, в городе [д'э́вушкъ, гъвъ́р'ит, в го́ръд'ь] *the girl, he says, is in the town*.

There are, however, a few words (most of them of one syllable) which are *never* stressed and in which, therefore, the vowels are always of the unstressed type. Such words are ведь [в'ьт'], бы [бы] or [бъ], ли [л'и], же [жы] or [жъ], что [штъ],[2] чтобы [штъбы],

---

[1] Pre-revolutionary.

[2] With the meaning 'that' (conjunction). что meaning 'what' is pronounced [што].

да [дъ]¹ and the two post-fixed particles -то [тъ] and -ка [къ]. The word и *and* frequently occurs without stress. The words a *and, but,* но *but,* он *he,* она *she,* оно *it,* они *they* and то ... то ... *now ... now ...* are usually unstressed but the vowels have more or less the same quality as if the words were stressed; она, оно and они having the second syllable stressed when spoken in isolation. но may be heard in the form [нъ], but *never* [на], even if the following syllable is stressed: Но дядя не понимал *but uncle didn't understand* is pronounced either [но д'а́д'ъ] etc. or [нъ д'а́д'ъ] etc., but *not* [на д'а́д'ъ] etc.

The words я *I,* ты *thou,* мы *we,* вы *you* are also unstressed usually, especially if used in conjunction with a verb. я is then pronounced [йа], with the unstressed vowel [а], never [йъ]. Thus: Я не понимал [йа н'ъпън'има́л] *I didn't understand.*

The last sentence illustrates the fact that the word не is usually unstressed and therefore pronounced [н'ь]. There are, however, some cases when (apart, of course, from purposes of emphasis) не is stressed. Thus, with certain forms of the past tense of the verbs быть *to be* and дать *to give*: не был [н'э́был], не было [н'э́былъ], не были [н'э́был'и], but не была [н'ьбыла́]; не дал [н'э́дъл], не дало [н'э́дълъ], не дали [н'э́дъл'и], but не дала [н'ьдала́].² не is also stressed in such complexes as не с кем [н'э́ с к'э́м], не о чем [н'э́ а чо́м], не у кого [н'э́ у каво́],³ the word after the preposition having a secondary stress. Since the principal or only stress in the examples in this paragraph falls in most cases on the word не it is necessary to provide it with a stress-mark in the phonetic transcriptions, though monosyllables, even when stressed, are not usually provided with a stress-mark in this book.

Similarly, ни is usually unstressed, whether it be an emphatic particle, an emphatic negative particle or part of the complex ни ... ни ... *neither ... nor ....* Note how the following phrases are pronounced: что ни есть духу [што́н'ийьс'(т')ду́ху] *as fast as ... could,* во что бы то ни стало [ваштобытън'и ста́лъ] *at any*

----

¹ With the meaning 'and', 'but', 'oh', etc., or 'let', 'may' (Да будет так! Да здравствует народ!), whereas да meaning 'yes' is always stressed and is pronounced [да].

² As can be seen from some of the transcriptions, when не is stressed with these verbs the verbs themselves have no stress at all.

³ As in such sentences as Ему не с кем говорить *He has nobody to talk to,* etc.

cost, ни шагу дальше [н'ишáгу дáл'шы] *not a step further*, ни отца ни матери не было там [н'иатцá н'имáт'ьр'и н'эбылъ там] *neither father nor mother was there.* An exception to this is ни, with the past tense of the verb быть, as an emphatic particle, in such phrases as во что бы то ни было [ваштóбытъ н'йбылъ] *at any cost*, где бы он ни был [гд'эбы он н'йбыл] *wherever he might be.*

A number of simple and common prepositions are usually not stressed but are treated as part of a phonetic unit with the following word. Thus: из города [изгóрълъ] *out of the town*, от брата [адбрáтъ] *from the brother*, ото всех [атафс'эх] *from everybody*, ко мне [камн'э] *to me*, со мной [самнóй] *with me*, со второго [съфтарóвъ] *from the second*, во мне [вамн'э] *in me*, во-вторых [въфтарыx] *secondly*, над горами [нъдгарáм'и] *above the mountains*, надо мной [нъдамнóй] *above me*, под окном [пъдакнóм] *beneath the window*, подо мной [пъдамнóй] *under me*, о чем [ачóм] *about what*, об отце [абатцэ] *about father*, обо всех [абафс'эх] *about everybody*, из-за стула [иззастýлъ] *from behind the chair*, из-за стола [иззъсталá] *from behind the table*, из-под стула [испатстýлъ] *from under the chair*, из-под стола [испътсталá] *from under the table*, передо мной [п'ьр'ьдамнóй] *in front of me.*

The prepositions через *through, across* and перед[1] *in front of* may be either unstressed or stressed: через окно [чьр'ьзакнó] or [чéр'ьс акнó],[2] перед домом [п'ьр'ьддóмъм] or [п'éр'ьт дóмъм].[2]

A few monosyllabic prepositions, when used in conjunction with certain words, draw the accent from the following word: the preposition and the following word are still treated as a phonetic unit but the stress is on the preposition, the vowel(s) of the following word being quite unstressed. This happens most frequently with на, less frequently with за, still less frequently with по, под and из, and in one or two expressions with от, без, о and со. The following are some of the commoner examples:

на:

на гору [нáгъру] *up the mountain*, на зиму [нáз'иму] *for the winter*, на берег [нáб'ьр'ьк] *on to the shore*, на дом [нáдъм] *to take home, for home use*, на пол [нáпъл] *on to the floor*, на день [нáд'ьн'] *for the day*, на ночь [нáнъч] *for the night*; на with the

[1] As distinct from the form передо, which is always unstressed.
[2] Note that when the preposition has an independent stress the final consonant symbol has the value it normally has at the end of a word.

numbers 3, 5, 6, 7, 8, 9, 10, 40, 100[1] in the sense of 'at' 'for',
e.g. на пять [на́п'ьт'], на десять [на́д'ьс'ьт'] на сто [на́стъ].

за:

за воду [за́въду] *for water*, за зиму [за́з'иму] *during the past
winter*, за год [за́гът] *during a year, in the space of a year*, за город
[за́гъръ́т] *out of town (motion)*, за городом [за́гъръдъм] *out of
town (location)*, за нос [за́нъс] *by the nose*, за морем [за́мър'ьм]
overseas, нога за ногу [нага́ за́нъгу] *with legs crossed*, за полночь
[за́пълнъч] *beyond midnight*.

по:

по морю [по́мър'у] *by sea*, по полю [по́пъл'у] *through the field*,
по лесу [по́л'ьсу] *through the wood*.

под:

под гору [по́дгьру] *down-hill*, под носом [по́днъсъм] *under
one's nose*.

из:

из дому [и́здъму] *out of the house*, из лесу [и́з'л'ьсу] *out of the
wood*, из виду [и́зв'иду] *out of sight*.

от:

от роду [о́трьду] *from birth*, час от часу [час о́тчьсу] *from
hour to hour*.

без:

пропасть без вести [прапа́с'т' б'е́з'в'ьс'т'и] *to disappear, go
missing*, без толку [б'э́стълку] *without sense*.

о (об):

бок о бок [бок о́бък] *side by side*, рука об руку [рука́ о́бруку]
hand in hand.

со:

со смеху [со́см'ьху] *with laughing*, со ста [со́стъ] *from a hundred*.

Note also во-время [во́вр'ьм'ъ] *in time* (*as distinct from* во
время [ва вр'е́м'ъ] *at the time of*).

In a number of long words in Russian there may occur a secondary stress in addition to the main stress. This secondary stress is
weaker than the main stress but its presence is clearly revealed by
the fact that vowel letters occurring in the position of secondary

[1] The stress is transferred from these numbers to the prepositions за
and по also.

stress have the phonetic value[1] that they have in stressed position. Thus the first e in самолетостроение *aircraft-construction* has the value that it has in самолет *aircraft*. Furthermore, the position of the secondary stress determines the quality of the other vowels in the part of a word where the secondary stress occurs just as in a word with one stress the position of the stress determines the value not only of the stressed vowel but of the other vowels also. Hence самолетостроение is pronounced [съмал'òтъстраéн'йь] (ср. самолет [съмал'óт]).

The secondary stress, where it occurs, always precedes the main stress in Russian. In this respect, the situation is something like that in English when adjective and noun occur together: in a phrase like *electric welding* there are two stresses but the stress on *electric* is weaker than the stress on *welding*. Russian электро-сварка (*electric welding*), if pronounced with secondary stress, as is permissible, will show the same relationship of secondary and main stresses: [ьл'òктръсвáркъ] (with one stress only this word would be pronounced [ьл'ьктрасвáркъ]).

It is not possible to establish any hard and fast rule concerning the occurrence of secondary stress. In general, it may be said that long, compound words of recent origin, especially technical words, may have a secondary accent: картòфелекопáлка[2] *potato-harvester*, мòтодивѝзия *motorised division*, морòзоустóйчивый *frost-resistant*, гàзогенерáтор *gas-generator*.

The prefixes после-, сверх- and the modern 'technical' prefixes архи-, анти-, ультра-, супер-, транс-, контр-, про-[3] are frequently found with secondary accent. Thus: пòслеледникóвый *post-glacial*, пòслеоперациóнный[4] *post-operational*, свèрхъестéственный[5] *supernatural*, ỳльтракорóткий *ultra-short*, ỳльтрафиолéтовый *ultra-violet*, трàнсатлантѝческий *trans-Atlantic*, кòнтрнаступлéние *counter-attack*, прòанглѝйский *pro-English*.

темно- and светло- as prefixes with adjectives of colour may be found with secondary stress or without stress. Hyphenated words have secondary stress on the first part.

[1] Except that [o] and [ə] do not have the slight diphthongal tendency (the final [ъ]-element) that they normally have when stressed (Chapter 3).
[2] For the rest of this section examples are quoted in spelling forms only, with stress-marks added.
[3] The native Russian prefix про does not take a secondary stress.
[4] But послеобéденный *post-prandial*, since this is of longer standing and less technical.   [5] The hard sign indicates hard [x] followed by [й].

Tertiary stress may also occur—in compounds made up of three parts. In such words the first stress will be stronger than the second, though weaker than the third: тѐплоэлѐктроцентра́ль *thermo-electric power-station*, мо̀товѐлого́нки *motor-cycle races*.

(b) The Pronunciation of Certain Types of Words and Grammatical Endings

(i) Contracted Compounds and Initial-Words

Since 1917 there has been in Russian a proliferation of such words as колхоз *collective farm*, партбилет *party membership card*, сельсовет *village soviet*, рабкор *workers' correspondent*, комсомол *Communist Party Youth Organisation*, etc. etc. Such words may be called 'contracted compounds', since they are compound words and at least one part is contracted (e.g. колхоз from коллективное хозяйство; партбилет from партийный билет).

The majority of these words have a secondary accent, only the ones in commoner use being pronounced with a single stress. All the above examples are single-stress words.

Tertiary stress may also be found on the compounds made up of more than two elements: Ми́нпѝщепро́м *Ministry of Food Industries*.

It should be noted, too, that, when a consonant letter occurs before и as a result of forming such contracted compounds, such a letter usually represents a hard consonant, not a soft consonant. Thus госиздат [гъсызда́т] *State Publishing House*, губисполком [губыспалко́м] *Provincial Executive Committee*.

Initial-words are, as the term indicates, words composed of the initial letters of the names of organisations and institutions, e.g. СССР, мтс, КПСС, Тасс, нэп, вуз, МГУ, etc. They fall into two groups from the point of view of pronunciation. The first group comprises those in which the letters have the normal value that they have in ordinary words, e.g. Тасс [тас] *Telegraph Agency of the Soviet Union*, вуз [вус] *Higher Educational Establishment*, нэп [нэп] *New Economic Policy*. The second group, by far the larger, comprises those whose pronunciation consists of the names of the letters which form them, e.g. СССР [эсэсэсэ́р] *U.S.S.R.*, КПСС [капээсэ́с] *Communist Party of the Soviet Union*, мтс [эмтээ́с] *Motor-Tractor Station*, ЦК [цэка́] *Central Committee*, РСФСР [эрэсэфэсэ́р] *Russian Socialist Federative Soviet Republic*,

МВД [эмвэдэ́] *Ministry of Internal Affairs.* In the pronunciation of these words the stress is always on the last syllable, consonants are not soft before [э], the vowels in the unstressed syllables have the quality of stressed vowels though [э] itself lacks the diphthongal quality described in Chapter 3: it consists simply of the first part of the slightly diphthongal sound described there.[1]

(ii) *Foreign Words*

In the last two or three hundred years, particularly since 1917, Russian has adopted a large number of words from Western European languages, principally French and English. It would perhaps be true to say that the majority of these words are now entirely 'Russified', but a very large number are not entirely Russified: the rules governing the relation between spelling and pronunciation are modified in these words, though the sounds used are entirely Russian. This applies both to words which are simply transliterated from foreign languages (e.g. радио) and to words which, when adopted, are provided with Russian grammatical endings (e.g. дегенерация).

The two words just quoted illustrate two of the principal ways in which foreign words which have not been entirely Russified differ in their pronunciation from ordinary Russian words, viz. the pronunciation of the letter o in unstressed position as [o] (instead of [a] or [ъ]) and the lack of softening of consonants occurring before the letter e. Of the two phenomena, the latter affects more words than does the former. The consonants most commonly concerned are [т], [д], [н], [с], [з], [р], and of these hard [т] and [д] are perhaps commonest before e in foreign words. Consonants made with the lips are sometimes affected by this phenomenon and are pronounced hard before e, while the remaining consonants are not affected at all.[2]

The following are some commoner examples of words where hard lip-consonants, [н], [с], [з] and [р] occur before e: мер [мэр] *mayor*, пер [пэр] *peer*, консоме [консомэ́] *consommé*, энергия

---

[1] A grammatical note may be added here: initial-words of the first types [Тасс, вуз, etc.] are declined (e.g. у Тасса, в вузе) whereas initial-words of the second type are not declined (в СССР, у КПСС).

[2] Note particularly that к, г and х represent soft consonants before e: пакет [пак'э́т] *packet*, богема [баг'э́мъ] *bohemianism*, схема [сх'э́мъ] *scheme, plan*.

[ьнэ́рг'ийъ] *energy*, тоннель [тонэ́л'] *tunnel*, сепсис [сэ́пс'ис] *sepsis*, асептический [асьпт'ичьск'ий] *antiseptic*, сентиментализм [сьн'т'им'ьнтал'йзм] *sentimentalism*, зеро [зэро́] *zero*, кабаре [кабарэ́] *cabaret*, рейс [рейс] *route, sailing, flight*, амнезия [амнэ́з'ийъ] *amnesia*, вальдшнеп [вал'тшнэ́п] *woodsnipe*, генетика [г'ьнэ́т'икъ] or [г'энэ́т'икь] *genetics*.

Examples with hard [т] and [д] before e are so numerous that it is not practicable to compile a short list of such words. It may be said that the prefixes де-, дез- and интер- are commonly (though not in all words) pronounced with hard [д] and [т].[1]

The letter e after another vowel letter usually indicates that the vowel represented by e is preceded by [й], which, in quick pronunciation, may be very faint or disappear altogether. In some foreign words [й] is not normally pronounced here: диета [д'иэ́тъ] *diet*, but гиена [г'ийэ́нъ] *hyena*, though the [й] is weak.

In many foreign loan-words where e and э occur in unstressed position they represent a vowel with distinct [e] or [э] quality, somewhat further back, however, than stressed [e] and [э]. This is particularly noticeable in the initial unstressed syllable.

Some common examples of foreign words pronounced with unstressed [о] are: радио [ра́д'ио] *radio*, радиоприемник [ра̀д'ио-пр'ийо́мн'ик] *radio-receiver*, доссье [дос'йэ́] *dossier*, консоме [консомэ́] *consommé*, коммюнике [ком'ю̈н'икэ́] *communiqué*. In such cases [о] does not have the slight diphthongal tendency described in Chapter 3.

In general, it can be said that the more narrowly technical a foreign word is (i.e. the less likely to be found out of a purely technical context), the more likely it is to have one or more of the features of pronunciation described in this section.

(iii) *Proper Names*

It is customary to address a Russian, even on a very slight acquaintance, by his or her first name and patronymic (Александр Сергеевич, Наталья Дмитриевна). Such forms of address are

[1] A very useful guide to the pronunciation of hard [д] and [т] before [e] is the pronouncing dictionary edited by R. I. Avanesov and S. I. Ozhegov: Русское литературное ударение и произношение, Moscow, 1955. It must be pointed out, however, that some of the distinctions in this dictionary seem artificial: it is, for example, rather odd, to say the least, to recommend hard [д] and [н] in дегенерация and дегенерировать but soft [д'] and [н'] in дегенеративный and дегенеративность.

spoken in parenthesis, as it were, and are often somewhat slurred so that some of the rules governing the relationship of spelling and pronunciation are not observed. Consonants and entire syllables (particularly ов and ев in patronymics) are omitted and the letter и following elided ов represents [ы]. Examples are: Александр Александрович [ал'ькса̀н-са́ныч], Михаил Павлович [м'иха̀л-па́лыч], Анна Ивановна [а̀ннъ-ива́ннъ] or [а̀нныва́ннъ], Эмилия Борисовна [ьм'ѝл'йъ-бар'йснъ], Софья Павловна [со̀ф'йъпа́лнъ], Павел Борисович [па̀л-бар'йсыч], Алексей Андреевич [ал'ькс'ѐйандр'е́ич].

(iv) *Two Grammatical Endings*

Genitive singular (m. and n.) of adjective and pronoun.

In the endings ого and его the letter г has the value of [в]. г also has the value of [в] in a few words where it is etymologically part of the ending ого or его: сегодня [с'ьво́д'н'ъ] *today,* итого [итаво́] *altogether, in sum,* сеголетка [с'ьво̀л'э́ткъ] *small fish less than one year old.*

The reflexive particles ся and сь.

Formerly с in these particles was pronounced as hard [с] in most forms in which the particles occurred. Nowadays с is pronounced as soft [с'] in many cases where ся and сь occur.

After т and ть the с in ся represents hard [с] and in the case of ть the soft sign has no effect on the preceding т: смеяться [с'м'ьйа́тсъ] *to laugh.* In rapid speech the [тс] of forms such as the one quoted may be reduced to [ц]: смеяться [с'м'ьйацъ], боится [байцъ] *he is afraid.*

After vowels and [й] the с in the reflexive particles ся and сь is soft: боюсь [байу́с'] *I fear,* собираетесь [съб'ира́ит'ьс'] *you intend,* не смейся [н'ьс'м'ейс'ъ] *don't laugh,* взялись [вз'ьл'йс'] *set to,* делаясь [д'э́лъйьс']¹ *becoming,* собравшись [сабра́фшыс'] *having prepared.*

After с and з it is considered better to pronounce с as hard [с] in the reflexive particle ся: понесся [пан'о́ссъ] *swept off,* расползся [распо́лссъ] *fell apart.*

After other consonants the reflexive particle now usually has soft [с'], though hard [с] is also found: боялся [байа́лс'ъ] (and [байа́лсъ]) *feared,* смеемся [с'м'ьйо́мс'ъ] (and [с'м'ьйо́мсъ]) *we*

¹ The second [ь] may be replaced by [ɛ] or a sound very like it, because of the surrounding soft consonants.

laugh, делаешься [д'э́лъишс'ъ] (and [д'э́лъишсъ]) *you become,*
отрекся [атр'э́кс'ъ] (and [атр'э́ксъ]) *renounced,* беречься
[б'ьр'е́чс'ъ] (and [б'ьр'е́чсъ]) *to beware.*

(v) *Numerals*

The Russian number-words are rather long, many of them having
three or four syllables even in the nominative case. Cases other than
the nominative may involve the addition of one or even two more
syllables (e.g. семьдесят - семидесяти) and long, compound numbers produce unwieldy, polysyllabic phrases. As a result of this,
Russian speakers, when using numbers in conversation or even
when reading out numbers, tend to omit sounds or whole syllables
from the numbers. The following are illustrations of the commoner
omissions and modifications: четыре [чты́р'ь], десять [д'ес'т'],
десяти [д'ьс'т'и́], одинадцать [ад'и́нцът'], двадцать [два́цът'],
двадцати[двъц^ьт'й],[1]тридцать[тр'йцат'], тридцати[тр'иц^ьт'й],[1]
пятьдесят[п'ьд'ьс'а́т], пятидесяти [п'ьт'йд'ьс'т'и], шестьдесят
[шыз'д'ьс'я́т],[2]шестидесяти[шыс'т'йд'ьс'т'и],[2]семьдесят[с'ем-
'д'ьс'т], восемьдесять [во́с'ьм'д'ьс'т], шесть сот [шыссо́т],
тысяча [ты́ш'чъ] or [ты́ш'ш'ъ].

In front of other numbers, тысяча is abbreviated still further to
[тыш'ч], [тыш'ш'] and even [тыш'], e.g. тысяча пять сот
тридцать четыре [тыш' п'ьт'со́т тр'йц^ьт' чты́р'ь], wherein the
last two elements may be further reduced to [тр'ицчты́р'ь]. In
the appropriate circumstances the final sound of [тыш'] may be
replaced by its voiced counterpart: в тысяча девять сот пятьдесят восьмом году [фтыж' д'ьв'т'со́т п'ьд'ьс'а́т вас'мо́м гаду́].

---

[1] With a suggestion of the vowel [ъ] (not [а]) after the [ц], or no vowel
at all here.
[2] [ы] here is very close to [ь] in quality.

PASSAGES FOR READING PRACTICE

1

Это было на даче. Я сидел на складном стуле
[э́тъ бы́лъ нада́чь. йа с'ид'э́л нъскладно́м сту́л'ь]

перед рыбачьим домиком, в котором жил. Недалеко
[п'ьр'ьдрыба́чйим до́м'икъм, фкато́ръм жыл. н'ьдъл'ько́]

от меня играла соседская девочка. Я только знал, что
[атм'ьн'а́ игра́лъ сас'э́цкъйъ д'э́въчкъ. йа то́л'къ знал, штъ]

ее зовут Лесик, а больше ничего о ней не знал.
[йьйо́ заву́т л'о́с'ик, а бо́л'шы н'ичьво́ ан'ей н'ьзна́л.]

Она была вся в веснушках и очень серьезная. Она
[ана́ была́ фс'а в'в'ьсну́шкъх и о́чьн' с'ьр'йо́знъйъ. ана́]

всегда играла одна. Ее мать подошла ко мне и сказала –
[фс'ьгда́ игра́лъ адна́. йьйо́ мат' пъдашла́ камн'э и сказа́лъ]

— Я пойду на почту в соседнюю деревню. Мне
[— йа пайду́ напо́чту фсас'е́д'н'уйу д'ьр'ев'н'у. мн'э]

некого попросить посмотреть за Лесиком, пока я
[н'э́къвъ пъпрас'и́т' пъсматр'е́т' зал'о́с'икъм, пака́ йа]

хожу. Могу я вас попросить посмотреть за девочкой?
[хажу́. магу́ йа вас пъпрас'и́т' пъсматр'е́т' зад'э́въчкъй?]

Я сказал — С удовольствием. Я люблю маленьких
[йа сказа́л — судавол'с'в'ийьм. йа л'убл'у́ ма́л'ьн'к'их]

девочек. Я даже умею рассказывать сказки.
[д'э́въчьк. йа да́жы ум'е́йу расска́зывът' скаск'и.]

— Вот и хорошо! сказала мать Лесика, и позвала ее.
[— во́ты хърашо́! сказа́лъ мат' л'о́с'икъ, и пъзвала́ йьйо́.]

Девочка подошла и сказала — Здравствуйте!
[д'э́въчкъ пъдашла́ и сказа́лъ — здра́с'т'ь!]

— Лесик, сказала ей мать, — пока я хожу, ты будешь
[— л'о́с'ик, сказа́лъ йей мат', — пака́ йа хажу́, ты бу́д'ьш]

играть здесь, и никуда не уйдешь, а тебе расскажут
[играт' з'д'ес', и н'икуда́ н'ь уйд'о́ш, а т'ьб'ə́ расска́жут]

сказки . . .
[ска́ск'и . . .]

— Кто мне расскажет сказки? спросила живо Лесик.
[— кто мн'ь расска́жыт ска́ск'и? спрас'илъ жы́въ л'о́с'ик.]

— Я никого не вижу.
[— йа н'икаво́ н'ьв'и́жу.]

— Я тебе расскажу сказки, сказал я.
[— йа́ т'ьб'ə́ ръсскажу́ ска́ск'и, сказа́л йа.]

Девочка взглянула на меня внимательно и ничего
[д'ə́въчкъ взгл'ьну́лъ нъм'ьн'а́ внима́т'ьл'нъ и н'ичьво́]

не сказала.
[н'ьсказа́лъ.]

Н. Тихонов
[эн т'и́хънъф]

2

Корчагин охватил голову руками и тяжело
[карча́г'ин ахват'и́л го́лъву рука́м'и и т'ьжыло́]

задумался. Перед его глазами пробежала вся его
[заду́мълс'ъ. п'ьр'ьдйьво́ глаза́м'и пръб'ьжа́лъ фс'а йьво́]

жизнь, с детства и до последних дней. Хорошо ли,
[жыз'н', з'д'э́цтвъ и дъпас'л'е́д'н'их д'н'ей. хърашо́л'и,]

плохо ли он прожил свои двадцать четыре года?
[пло́хъл'и он про́жыл свай два́цът' чты́р'ь го́дъ?]

Перебирая в памяти год за годом, проверял свою
[п'ьр'ьб'ира́йа фпа́м'ьт'и гот заго́дъм, пръв'ьр'а́л свайу́]

жизнь, как беспристрастный судья, и с глубоким
[жыз'н', как б'ьспр'истра́сны суд'йа, и зглубок'им]

удовлетворением решил, что жизнь прожита не так
[удъвл'ьтвар'е́н'ийьм р'ьшы́л, штъ жыз'н' пръжыта́ н'ь так]

уж плохо. Но было не мало ошибок, сделанных
[уш пло́хъ. но бы́лъ н'ь ма́лъ ашы́бък, з'д'э́лъных]

по дури, по молодости, а больше всего по незнанию.
[паду́р'и, памо́лъдъс'т'и, а бо́л'шы фс'ьво́ пън'ьзна́н'ийу.]

Самое главное — не проспал горячих дней, нашел
[са́мъйь гла́внъйь — н'ь прасп́а́л гар'а́чих д'н'ей, нашо́л]

свое место в железной схватке за власть, и на багряном
[свайо́ м'э́стъ вжыл'э́знъй схва́тк'ь завла́с'т', и нъбагр'а́нъм]

знамени революции есть и его несколько капель
[зна́м'ьн'и р'ьвал'у́цыйи йес'т' и йьво́ н'э́скъл'къ ка́п'ьл']

крови.
[кро́в'и.]

Н. Островский
[эн астро́фск'и]

3

С Карпат на Украину
[скарпа́т наукра́йну]

Пришел солдат небритый,
[пр'ишо́л салда́т н'ьбр'и́тый,]

Его шинель в лохмотьях,
[йьво́ шын'е́л' влахмо́т'йъх,]

И сапоги разбиты.
[и съпаг'и́ разб'и́ты.]

Пропахший мглой ночлегов
[прапа́хшы мглой начл'ə́гъф]

И горячью махорки,
[и го́р'ьчйу махо́рк'и,]

С георгиевской медалью
[зг'ьо́рг'ийьфскъй м'ьда́л'йу]

На рваной гимнастерке,
[нарва́нъй г'имнас'т'о́рк'ь,]

Он встал перед простором
[он фстал п'ьр'ьтпрасто́ръм]

На брошенном погосте.
[набро́шынъм паго́с'т'ь.]

Четыре ветра кличут
[чьты́р'ь в'ə́тръ кл'и́чут]

К себе солдата в гости.
[кс'ьб'ə́ салда́тъ вго́с'т'и.]

Э. Г. Багрицкий
[э г'ə́ багр'и́цки]

4

Орбита первого советского спутника представляет
[арб'и́тъ п'э́рвъвъ сав'э́цкъвъ спу́т'н'икъ пр'ьцтавл'а́ит]

собой эллипс, один из фокусов которого находится
[сабо́й эл'и́пс, ад'и́н исфо́кусъф като́ръвъ нахо́д'ицъ]

в центре Земли. Высота полета спутника в связи
[фцэ́нтр'ь з'ьм'л'и́. высата́ пал'о́тъ спу́т'н'икъ фс'в'ьз'и́]

с этим не постоянна, а периодически изменяется,
[сэ́т'им н'ь пъстайа́ннъ, а п'ьр'иад'и́чьск'и изм'ьн'а́ицъ,]

достигая максимума около 900 километров.
[дъс'т'ига́йъ мъкс'иму́мъ о́къл д'ьв'ьт'й сот к'илам'э́тръф.]

Апогей орбиты (наивысщая точка) паходится в Южном
[апаг'е́й арб'и́ты (наивы́шшъйъ то́чкъ) нахо́д'ицъ вйу́жнъм]

полушарии   Земли,   а   перигей   (наинизшая
[пълуша́р'ии   з'ьм'л'и́,   а   п'ьр'иг'е́й   (наин'и́шшъйъ]

точка)   —   в   Северном   полушарии.   Плоскость
[то́чкъ)   —   фс'е́в'ьрнъм   пълуша́р'ии.   пло́скъс'т']

орбиты наклонена к плоскости земного экватора
[арб'и́ты нъклън'ьна́ кпло́скъс'т'и з'ьмно́въ эква́търъ]

на   65°.   В связи с этим
[нъшыз'д'ьс'а́т   п'а́т'   гра́дусъф.   фс'в'ьз'и́   сэ́т'им]

траектория спутника проходит над всеми районами
[трайькто́р'ийъ спу́т'н'икъ прахо́д'ит натфс'е́м'и райо́нъм'и]

Земли,   находящимися   приблизительно   между
[з'ьм'л'и́,   нъхад'а́ш'ш'им'ис'ъ   пр'ибл'из'и́т'ьл'нъ   м'э́жду]

Северным   и   Южным   полярными   кругами.
[с'е́в'ьрным   и   йу́жным   пал'а́рным'и   круга́м'и.]

"Наука и жизнь"
[нау́къ и жыз'н']

SELECT BIBLIOGRAPHY

R. I. Avanesov, Русское литературное произношение, Moscow, 1950.

R. I. Avanesov, Фонетика современного русского литературного языка, Moscow, 1956.

R. I. Avanesov and S. I. Ozhegov, Русское литературное ударение и произношение - Опыт словаря-справочника, Moscow, 1955.

S. C. Boyanus, *A Manual of Russian Pronunciation*, London, 1944.

S. C. Boyanus, *Russian Pronunciation and Russian Phonetic Reader*, London, 1955.